Lord Jesus, I Want To See...

Family/Children Edition

Reverend Peter G. Vu

My Own Book of Bible Stories (More than fifty favorites, especially chosen and retold for Young Children) by Pat Alexander, illustrated by Carolyn Cox.

The Book of God for Children by Walter Wangerin, Jr.

First published by Dog Ear Publishing
4011 Vincennes Rd
Indianapolis, IN 46268
www.dogearpublishing.net

ISBN: 978-1-4575-5433-9

This book is printed on acid-free paper.

Printed in the United States of America

I dedicate this book to the following:

- My Parishioners: Many children (my Little Friends) and families, who have let me be a part of their lives and faith journey and to see their daily struggles have added real flavor to my prayer life, as I try to remember them often in my daily prayers.
- My Family: Grandparents, parents, uncles, and aunts, who first taught me how to pray and laid the foundation for me to build a strong and faithful prayer life.
- My Teachers: Priests, religious brothers and sisters, deacons, catechists, and laypeople, who lifted my prayer life to a higher level and gave it depth and tradition but also challenged me to pray often.
- My Friends: These dear souls have helped and encouraged me with this project.

Thank you, and God bless you all.
You are in my thoughts often and my prayers always.

Introduction

Prayer is an essential part of our Christian life. I grew up in a time that the Church asked its members, especially its young, to memorize many prayers. In fact, one of the requirements for a child to receive a sacrament in the old days was to learn and remember a handful of prayers. If someone could not recite the required prayers, this person would not be able to receive a particular Sacrament. Holding back on a Sacrament is not only a warning for a child about the importance of preparation, but also a way to emphasize the valuable role of the Sacraments in the life of a Christian and the Church.

Unfortunately, many Children and families today do not seem to appreciate the reception of the Sacraments and their blessings in their lives. In addition, Christians these days do not take their prayer life seriously; hence, they do not try to memorize traditional prayers. Most children of this generation are busy with sports, computer games, friends, and social life. Moreover, many children do not grow up in a traditional family with loving parents or receive proper spiritual care that fosters a close relationship with Jesus. Also, they get bombarded with bad influences by our faith-free society and temptations by the power of darkness around them.

Realizing these challenges are facing our children, and hoping to give parents a hand in fostering a strong faith life and good prayer habits, I have written this ***Prayer Book for Children and Family***. It is designed for **children** to use during their own **weekly** prayers or for **families** to pray with their children as a unit. Readers can **start the week** by praying on **Sunday** with a **special topic**, reflecting on it with **a Bible story**, listening to **Jesus**

talk about it, and then practicing it with **a concrete action throughout the week.** For months with a **fifth week,** readers can go to the section at the end of the Prayer Book called "**The Fifth Week of the Month**" and use it as a regular month throughout the year. I have devised this new way of **weekly praying** that is **simple, personal, relatable, character-building,** and **suitable for a busy life** for our children and families in modern times.

This **weekly prayer book** not only helps our children and family begin the week on a right note, but also encourages them to work on specific topics and Christian attributes such as Friend, Teacher, Faith, Love, Generosity, Forgiveness, Thankfulness, and so on. If we have watched the news and had a personal encounter with our young, we must admit both the world at large and our youth in desperate need of character-building and moral guidance to help create good citizens and a healthy society for the next generation. Unfortunately, due to political correctness and other social trends, moral character and great personal attributes have taken a back seat to other qualities such as appearance, charm, glamour, fame, social status, and possessions. We must demand and encourage our children of this great nation and future generations to work on and acquire Christian attributes and other moral characteristics for the sake of their well-being and happiness. Finally, gone are the days that we can require our children to memorize and recite the traditional prayers.

After reflecting on what I shared above and seeing the needs of God's children in my twenty years of serving them and their families in parishes and ten years of seminary training, I have devised this format of praying, which is rooted in Holy Scriptures, daily topics, personal experiences, character-building, and practical spiritual exercises. The format is designed to be self-reflecting and easy reading. My hope is to help each child work on important qualities while spending time in the presence of Jesus. I chose the title of the book, "**Lord Jesus, I want to see...,**" after prayerfully reflecting on the miracles Jesus did for the public during His ministry and the problems our children face today. Like a blind, our children do not seem to see what is right or wrong in our confusing world these days. Furthermore, during my homilies, many children have told me that blindness would be much more difficult to endure compared to other problems such as being deaf, mute, paralyzed, afflicted with leprosy, and so on.

My hope is that our Lord Jesus will heal the spiritual blindness of our children and families and help them see things in their lives with a better vision. May they also grow closer to Him and acquire many wonderful personal qualities each day as they try to become better Christians in this challenging world.

Fr. Peter G. Vu

JANUARY

Lord Jesus, I Want to See...

Topic of the Week: Children

"And people were bringing children to Him [Jesus] that He might touch them; but the disciples rebuked them. When Jesus saw this, He became indignant and said to them, 'Let the children come to me; do not prevent them, for the Kingdom of God belongs to such as these. Amen, I say to you, whoever does not accept the Kingdom of God like a child will not enter it.' Then, He embraced them, blessed them, and placed His hands on them." (Mark 4:35-41)

My Talk with Jesus

Today's Bible passage is one of the favorite passages that people often use on the occasion of a child's Baptism. Without a doubt, Jesus loved children and had a special bond with them. They definitely have His ears and His heart. We wonder why children do not use that privilege and come to Jesus often to ask Him to help them and others as well. In fact, Jesus came to the rescue of some children during His years of ministry and healed them from sickness, even death. He showed them not only the love of God but also the miracles of Heaven.

What is it about children that bring out of the Lord Jesus His tender care and special attention for them? First, children have a simple faith. They do not place conditions on or bargain with Jesus for their belief in God. They do not write a big book to explain their faith or create complicated rituals to show their love for God. They simply trust in God. Second, they always have an upbeat attitude and hopeful spirit. For they believe that God will take care of them. Third, they do not hold grudges and can forgive easily. They might get mad at someone about something, but quickly forget about it. Fourth, they always have an open mind and are willing to try something new. They are open to the Holy Spirit to guide and show them different ways of thinking or feeling about something. Finally, they are usually honest in their thoughts and pure in their hearts. They always say what they think and tell how they feel. They do not hide their thoughts or feelings. Perhaps these are some of the reasons that make Jesus love children.

Lord Jesus, I want to see

Jesus, the Best Friend and Defender of Children, You call on everyone to become like children if they want to enter the Kingdom of God. Sometimes, I might ignore the great qualities above and let the world lure me into taking up some bad habits of an adult like swearing, smoking, or drinking. But, all those adult things will get me into a lot of trouble and harm my relationship with you and my family. I certainly do not want to do that. All the fun in the world will come to an end at some point. However, my family and you will always be there for me through all the good and bad times of my life until the end of my life. The best way for me to stay close to you and keep these relationships strong is to work on the fine qualities of a child every day. Most important, I must make good use of your love for children. I must come to you often in prayer to share my needs and the requests of others like my family and unfortunate people around me. That is an honor I should be proud of and use more regularly so that many people can meet you and find you in their lives.

My Promise

This week, I will come to you, Lord, in prayer and ask for the needs of my family, friends, cousins, grandparents, aunts, uncles, or some unfortunate people that I have learned about on the news. As a child, I know I have your ears and heart to hear my prayers. Thank you, Jesus, the Best Friend and Defender of Children. I love you!

Topic of the Week: Healing

"They came to Jericho. And as He [Jesus] was leaving Jericho with His disciples and a sizeable crowd; Bartimaeus, a blind man, son of Timaeus, sat by the roadside begging. Upon hearing that it was Jesus of Nazareth, he began to cry out and say, 'Jesus, Son of David, have pity on me.' Jesus stopped and said, 'Call him.' So, they called the blind man, saying to him, 'Take courage; get up, He [Jesus] is calling you.' He threw aside his cloak, sprang up, and came to Jesus. Jesus said to him in reply, 'What do you do want me to do for you?' The blind man replied to Him, 'Master, I want to see.' Jesus told him, 'Go your way; your faith has saved you.' Immediately, he received his sight and followed Jesus on the way." (Mark 10:46-52)

My Talk with Jesus

It is amazing how Jesus healed the blind man! I have asked many children about what illness would be the worst for someone to endure. Keep in mind that Jesus healed the blind, the deaf, the mute, the leper, the possessed, the paralytic, the sick, and many others. Most children have said that the worst suffering anyone might ever have to endure is blindness, because the person would not be able to see anything. For them, there is nothing worse in this life than not being able to see. They believe everyone should be able to endure and survive other physical and mental problems except losing one's vision. If we can see, we are able to do anything. Hence, Bartimaeus' request to Jesus: "Master, I want to see" is what this prayer book is all about. It means we all need to have a good spiritual vision to make it through this life.

Most of us can only imagine the suffering that someone must endure from the loss of vision or any kind of sickness. It is not fun to be in pain or suffer any form of illness and disease. Jesus certainly feels badly for anyone who is sick or suffering. During His ministry, He did not hesitate to reach out and try to heal them. Often, He would work on suffering patients even on the Sabbath Day, which is the day of rest according to Jewish tradition. Jesus certainly did not want them to suffer one moment longer. Hopefully, like Jesus, we have some compassion and care for suffering people around us, especially disabled folks. They might look, walk, or talk differently than we do. But, that does not mean we should laugh at them or make fun of them. Rather, we should reach out like Jesus did, befriend them, and help them feel loved and included.

Lord Jesus, I want to see

Jesus, Healer of Body, Mind, and Spirit; emotional pain is what many kids must deal with these days. This pain often arises from feeling rejected or being made fun of by their peers. Today, with the tool of social media, this form of suffering can increase a thousand times as people try to say the meanest or nastiest things about others behind the veil of the Internet. If I am a disciple of Jesus, I should not do that. I should find only the kindest or the nicest things to say to people around me. When I see some kid who feels alone or looks sad, I should walk up to him/her and try to comfort him/her somehow. Give me your compassionate heart and caring spirit so that I may always desire to bring healing and comfort to everyone around me.

My Promise

This week, I will reach out to a disabled person and help him/her, bring comfort to someone who might feel sad about something or try to include someone who might feel left out. Thank you, Jesus, Healer of Body, Mind, and Spirit. I love you!

Topic of the Week: Prayer

"He [Jesus] was praying in a certain place, and when He had finished, one of His disciples said to Him, 'Lord, teach us to pray just as John taught his disciples.' He said to them, 'When you pray, say: Father, hallowed be your name, your Kingdom come. Give us each day our daily bread and forgive us our sins for we ourselves forgive everyone in debt to us, and do not subject us to the final test.' And He said to them, 'Suppose one of you has a friend to whom he goes at midnight and says, 'Friend, lend me three loaves of bread, for a friend of mine has arrived at my house from a journey and I have nothing to offer him,' and he says in reply from within, 'Do not bother me; the door has already been locked and my children and I are already in bed. I cannot get up to give you anything.' I tell you, if he does not get up to give the loaves because of friendship, he will get up to give him whatever he needs because of his persistence.' And I tell you, ask and you will receive; seek and you will find; knock and the door will be open to you..." (Luke 11:1-13)

My Talk with Jesus

We pray The Lord's Prayer or The Our Father often, but most of us do not know how that prayer came about. The Scripture passage above helps us see how Jesus created it and taught His disciples that short and sweet prayer. Surely, prayer is important in the life of a Christian. Otherwise, the disciple would not have asked Jesus to teach him and others how to pray. Jesus knew the value of prayer and prayed often Himself as the Gospels tell us.

People usually came to Jesus back then to ask Him for something for themselves or someone else. Prayer has been used over the years to ask God for help. People often pray for their own needs, but they sometimes ask for God's help for somebody else. Have you ever come to Jesus to ask for something before? Many people find it difficult to keep praying when their prayers do not get answered the way they want. They might get mad at God for not granting them their prayer requests. On another occasion during His ministry, Jesus talked about prayer requests and reassured us that He will not give us a snake when we ask for a fish or a scorpion when we ask for an egg. God is not that mean or cruel to give us bad or evil things in answer to our prayer requests. Therefore, we should not blame God for the way our prayers are answered. God has a plan for everything; sometimes that plan might not make any sense to us. Only with time will we gradually understand and appreciate it much better. Yet, it is in our best interest to keep on praying and asking God for help.

Lord Jesus, I want to see

Jesus, the Hope and Answer of all Prayers, you called on your disciples to be persistent and not give up on praying, even when things got tough in their lives. You ask us to call out louder and knock on the door of God's house relentlessly if our prayer requests do not seem to be heard. You want us to have a close relationship with you through prayers. Like two best friends who never get sick of spending an awfully long time with each other on the phone, I should not get tired of spending a long time in prayer with you as your best friend forever (BFF). One of the best forms of prayer is thanksgiving and giving praise to God. I should give thanks daily for my health, family, friends, food, clothes, home, peaceful nation, freedom to practice my faith, a decent school to study and play sports, and all my other blessings.

My Promise

This week, I will give thanks to you, Lord, for being my BFF and for all good things in my life that you have given me. Thank you, Jesus, the Hope and Answer of all Prayers. I love you!

Topic of the Week: Sharing

"... A large crowd followed Him [Jesus], because they saw the signs He was performing on the sick. Jesus went up on the mountain, and there He sat down with His disciples... When Jesus raised His eyes and saw that a large crowd was coming to Him, He said to Philip, 'Where can we buy enough food for them to eat?' He said this to test him, because He Himself knew what He was going to do. Philip answered Him, 'Two hundred days' wages worth of food would not be enough for each of them to have a little bit.' One of His disciples, Andrew, the brother of Simon Peter, said to Him, 'There is a boy here who has five barley loaves and two fish; but what good are these for so many?' Jesus said, 'Have the people recline.'... The men reclined, about five thousand in number. Then, Jesus took the loaves, gave thanks, and distributed them to those who were reclining and also as much of the fish as they wanted. When they had their fill, He said to His disciples, 'Gather the fragments leftover, so that nothing will be wasted.' So, they collected them, and filled twelve wicker baskets with fragments from the five barley loaves that had been more than they could eat..." (John 6:1-15)

My Talk with Jesus

If we have ever thrown a party for thousands of people, we can appreciate what Jesus and His disciples had to do to take care of a big, hungry crowd. It is amazing how they fed the thousands without the crowd becoming angry or trampling on each other due to hunger. Rather, in the end, the disciples collected lots of leftovers after the crowd had their fill.

But, what fascinates us the most about this miracle, besides everything we just heard above, is the fact that Jesus did it using five barley loaves and two fish, which were given by a little boy. If that boy did not share these foods with the crowd, the miracle never would have happened. Jesus needed that boy and his generosity and kindness to make the miracle happen. Similarly, Jesus needs generous and kind folks in our time so He can make this miracle happen in our world daily and take care of the hungry and the poor. Perhaps we could imitate that boy and learn to share God's blessings for us with others if we want miracles like this to keep happening around us. Unfortunately, sharing does not come naturally for any of us. We might recall from growing up with our siblings about how we fight over everything, especially sharing things with others.

Lord Jesus, I want to see

Jesus, Generous Giver of all Gifts, imagine if the boy in the Bible story above did not want to share his loaves and fish with that hungry crowd? That would mean many people would go hungry and some might pass out along the way. Or, what would happen if Jesus did not want to share His life and gifts/talents with others? We would never have His amazing miracles and many lives being saved as we hear about in the Gospels. Unfortunately, many rich and famous folks in our world these days do not want to share God's abundant blessings generously with the misfortunate and the poor around them. This is why we have seen the number of homeless and poor continue to increase in our society. If many young people and I would learn to share God's blessings for us generously, our world would be changed for the better, and everyone would be able to experience the life of Heaven right here in this life.

My Promise

This week, I will try to share God's blessings for me with my family and the people around me gladly, without expecting anything in return. Thank you, Jesus, Generous Giver of all Gifts. I love you!

FEBRUARY

Lord Jesus, I Want to See...

Topic of the Week: Evil

"They brought Him [Jesus] a demoniac who was blind and mute. He cured the mute person so that He could speak and see. The crowd was astounded... When the Pharisees saw this, they said, 'This man drives out demons only by the power of Beelzebul, the Prince of demons.' But, He knew what they were thinking and said to them, 'Every Kingdom divided against itself will be laid waste, and no town or house divided against itself will stand. And if Satan drives out Satan, he is divided against himself; how then will his kingdom stand? And if I drive out demons by Beelzebul, by whom do your people drive them out? ... But, if it is by the Spirit of God that I drive out demons, then the Kingdom of God has come upon you...'" (Matthew 12:22-32)

My Talk with Jesus

Many people do not know where evil came from. The truth is that all evil begins in the Prince of Darkness, Devil, Satan, or Beelzebul. The main goal of that Prince is to create as much evil in the world as possible and try to drive us away from our loving Creator. Jesus confirms this for us in the Scripture passage and lets us know that this evil leader does not want any kind of division in his kingdom that might make it to fall apart. It is sad for us to see that the power of darkness and evil acts continue to increase in our country and around the world. People let anger and certain beliefs drive them to hurt innocent people without regret. Many even encourage and promote others to do harm to their neighbors, as if it is their important religious duty. Worst yet, some even want to worship the

Devil and pledge their allegiance to the Power of Darkness. How can anyone be that blind and let wicked people or certain feelings drive them to do evil and hurtful things to their neighbors? Or, how can someone desire and embrace death and destruction over life and growth?

All these bad things happen regularly in our world because evil is real, and it exists in our daily life. We have seen how kids got mad at their families and hurt them or how kids are treated badly by their friends and then decided to shoot people at their school. Or, we have heard about terrorist groups like ISIS, who hate people that do not fit with their way of thinking, especially Christians and Westerners, and hence carry out violent acts around the world. How can we deal with these wicked folks and their evil acts? Should we take revenge and do the same thing back to them?

Lord Jesus, I want to see

Jesus, the source of Goodness and Kindness, you call your disciples to love not only their neighbors but also their enemies. St. Paul agrees with that by saying: "Do not be overcome by evil, but overcome evil with good." (Romans 12:21) Joseph agreed with this by forgiving his brothers for the evil things they did to him and taking care of their needs when they came to him for help due to famine and hunger (Gen 37-50). Can I love my enemies and do good things for someone who has done evil things to me? It is certainly not easy to practice this in the face of evil, for we tend to give back the same thing people do to us. The world often says this about its justice system: "An eye for an eye, a tooth for a tooth." I must be better than the world and try to break that vicious cycle by doing good things instead of evil things in return. There is nothing good about evil; it is all pain, hurt, tears, and sadness.

My Promise

This week I will try to see what evil things I might have done to others. Then, I will ask God for forgiveness and pray for those victims. I will also pray that God will give me a heart filled with goodness, kindness, love, peace, and compassion. Thank you, Jesus, the source of Goodness and Kindness. I love you!

Topic of the Week: Forgiveness

"He [Jesus] said, 'A man had two sons, and the younger son said to his father, 'Father, give me the share of your estate that should come to me.' So, the father divided the property between them. After a few days, the younger son collected all his belongings and set off to a distant country where he squandered his inheritance on a life of dissipation. When he had freely spent everything, a severe famine struck that country, and he found himself in dire need. So, he hired himself out to one of the local citizens who sent him to his farm to ten the swine. And he longed to eat his fill of the pods on which the swine fed, but nobody gave him any. Coming to his senses he thought, 'How many of my father's hired workers have more than enough food to eat; but here am I, dying from hunger. I shall get up and go to my father and I shall say to him, 'Father, I have sinned against Heaven and against you. I no longer deserve to be called your son; treat me as you would treat one of your hired workers.' So, he got up and went back to his father. While he was still a long way off, his father caught sight of him, and was filled with compassion. He ran to his son, embraced him, and kissed him... Then, he ordered his servants, 'Quickly bring the finest robe and put it on him; put a ring on his finger and sandals on his feet. Take the fattened calf and slaughter it. Then, let us celebrate'... Now the older son had been out in the field and, on his way back, as he neared the house, he heard the sound of music and dancing... He became angry, and when he refused to enter the house, his father came out and pleaded with him... He said to him, 'My son, you are here with me always; everything I have is yours. But, now we must celebrate and rejoice because your brother was dead and has come to life again; he was lost and has been found.'" (Luke 15: 11-32)

My Talk with Jesus

One of the important themes that Jesus often discusses with us in the Gospels is forgiveness. This idea is easier said than done, because when someone does something wrong to us or hurts us, it takes a long time for us to forgive that person. That wound needs time and lots of prayers to be healed. Clearly, the father did not have any problem forgiving the younger son after everything he did. The reason he could do that was because of his abundant love and mercy for his children. On the contrary, his oldest son did not share the same feelings, but was full of judgment and condemnation. He was angry that his father could forgive his sinful brother that easily and did not make him pay for what he did. Instead, his sinful brother was given a big, welcome home party, which is something the older son was not allowed to have despite his good behaviors and hardworking nature. As we can see, it takes mercy and love to forgive someone.

Lord Jesus, I want to see

Jesus, Teacher and Model of Forgiveness, Peter came to you once and asked if seven times would be enough to forgive his brothers and sisters. You answered, "It is not just seven times, but it is seventy times seven times." In other words, you want us to never stop forgiving. You help us stay committed to that rule by forgiving everyone who hung you on the Cross and hence giving us your great example of forgiveness. Give me the strength and courage to forgive people who might have hurt or wronged me in the course of my life.

My Promise

This week I will look back to see if I still hold grudges against someone and, with prayers and God's help, I will slowly let go of past hurt and learn to forgive the person who wronged me. I will replace that hurt with your love and peace for me. Thank you, Jesus, Teacher and Model of Forgiveness. I love you!

Topic of the Week: Temptation

"Filled with the Holy Spirit, Jesus returned from the Jordan and was led by the Spirit into the desert for forty days, to be tempted by the Devil. He ate nothing during those days, and when they were over He was hungry. The Devil said to Him, 'If you are the Son of God, command this stone to become bread.' Jesus answered him, 'It is written: 'One does not live by bread alone.'' Then, the Devil took Him up and showed Him all the kingdoms of the world in a single instant. The Devil said to Him, 'I shall give you all this power and their glory; for it has been handed over to me, and I may give it to whomever I wish. All this will be yours, if you worship me.' Jesus said to him in reply, 'It is written: 'You shall worship the Lord, your God, and Him alone shall you serve.'' Then the Devil led Him to Jerusalem, made Him stand on the parapet of the Temple and said to Him, 'If you are the Son of God, throw yourself down from here, for it is written: 'He [God] will command His angels concerning you to guard you, and with their hands they will support you, lest you dash your foot against a stone.'' Jesus said to him in reply, 'It also says, 'You shall not put the Lord, your God, to the test.'' When the Devil had finished every temptation, he parted from Jesus for a time." (Luke 4: 1-13)

My Talk with Jesus

This Gospel passage shares with us how the Devil tempted the Lord on three things: food, worldly power and possessions, and faith in God. After spending forty days in the desert fasting and praying to prepare Himself for His upcoming Cross, Jesus was tired and hungry. So, the first thing the Devil tested

Him with was food. The Devil wanted Jesus to use His mighty power not to save and help others in need, but simply for Himself by turning a stone into bread. Jesus resisted the urge of hunger by letting the Devil know that a person depends not just on food but also God's grace and spiritual strength to live.

The second temptation that the Devil threw at Jesus was worldly power and possessions. The Devil took Jesus up on the highest mountain and promised to give Him all the kingdoms of the world and their glory if He would bow down and worship him. Jesus most certainly would not do that. The Devil forgot that the only one who receives any worship is God. Today, people search for five minutes of fame or possessions and hence put themselves amidst the temptations and control of the Devil.

The last temptation that the Devil tried on Jesus was to take Him to the steeple of the Temple and tell Him to throw Himself down if He believed in God, for the Bible says that God will be there to protect and help His believers. Jesus knew that God the Father would always watch out for Him, and He told the Devil to back off and have respect for God. We need to do the same when tempted.

Lord Jesus, I want to see

Jesus, Son of God and Savior of the World, the Devil even tempted you and searched for your weaknesses to control and lure you away from God the Father. Surely, we all get tempted daily over all kinds of things: hatred, fighting, doubt of God's love, envy, selfishness, greed, pride, lust, laziness, anger, gluttony, and hopelessness, to name just a few. I could be tempted to be mad at someone or not to share God's blessings for me with the people around me. But, you taught me to resist all the temptations and call on you to help me fight back so that the angels can gather to take care of me.

My Promise

This week I will think about my weaknesses that the Devil might use to tempt me, such as fighting with someone easily. With God's help, I will try not to get into a fight with someone even if I might be provoked. Thank you, Jesus, Son of God and Savior of the World. I love you!

Topic of the Week: Sorrow

"They came to a place named Gethsemane, and He [Jesus] said to His disciples, 'Sit here while I pray.' He took with Him Peter, James, and John, and began to be troubled and distressed. Then He said to them, 'My soul is sorrowful even to death. Remain here and keep watch.' He advanced a little and fell to the ground and prayed that if it were possible the hour might pass by Him; He said, 'Abba Father, all things are possible to you. Take this cup away from me, but not what I will but what you will.'" (Mark 14: 32-42)

My Talk with Jesus

It makes us cry when we read stories like this and learn that the soul of Jesus was full of sorrow as He prepared Himself for His suffering and death. But, this was not the first time we heard that Jesus was in sorrow. For example, when He saw people carrying the dead son of a widow out of town, He was moved with pity and said to her, "Do not weep." Then, he brought the deceased back to life and the crowd glorified God. (Mark 7:11-17) No doubt, pity and sorrow are emotions that Jesus did not lack.

In fact, the whole Bible is full of moments of sorrow. For the journey of God's people to the Promised Land in the Old Testament is full of sad moments and difficulties. They were driven out of their homes and into slavery many times. They lost not only their possessions but also their family members because of their invaders. They had to face hunger, thirst, drought, plagues, diseases, and other difficulties. Meanwhile, the journey of God's people to the Kingdom of Heaven in the

New Testament is full of tears and challenges too. They were persecuted for their faith and suffered all forms of torture. Many even lost their lives for being a Christian. They have also dealt with divorce, loss of job, health issues, tragedies, and so on. But, the Bible is not just about listing a bunch of sorrowful moments. It also shows us how God's people dealt with those moments. They did not let sad moments overwhelm them and turn into depression, because God's people are people of hope and faith. They were able to find hope and a new life from moments of sorrow and darkness. They knew that their God will come to their aid to comfort them, dry their tears, and help them find a new life. Like God's people, our life has many moments of sorrow: Loss of loved ones or a pet, being hurt by a friend or someone you know, having to deal with some disability, and so on. The challenge for us is how to overcome these moments of sorrow and turn them into a time of hope and a new life.

Lord Jesus, I want to see

Jesus, source of Comfort and Hope, you know how it feels to be in sorrow because you had moments of sadness during your time here on earth. Yet you did not let those feelings turn you into a sad, depressed, or angry person. Instead, you asked God the Father to give you the Spirit of comfort, peace, and hope so that you can bring the Good News to the hurting and the misfortunate. I might have sad moments or bad days. But, I should not let those moments pull me down and turn me away from you and people around me. Instead, I should come to you in prayer with my sadness and ask you to cheer me up with your love and peace. I should realize that you always want me to be happy and hopeful by giving me sunshine and a brand-new day.

My Promise

This week I will look for what has caused me to be in sorrow lately. Then, I will bring it to you, Lord, in prayer and ask you to help me be happy and be the joyful presence of Jesus to people around me. Thank you, Jesus, source of Comfort and Hope. I love you!

MARCH

Lord Jesus,
I Want to See...

Topic of the Week: Betrayal

"… When it was evening, He [Jesus] reclined at table with the Twelve. And while they were eating, He said, 'Amen, I say to you, one of you will betray me.' Deeply distressed at this, they began to say to Him one after another, 'Surely it is not I, Lord?' He said in reply, 'He who has dipped his hand into the dish with me is the one who will betray me. The Son of Man indeed goes, as it is written of Him, but woe to that man by whom the Son of Man is betrayed. It would be better for that man if he had never been born.' Then Judas, his betrayer, said in reply, 'Surely it is not I, Rabbi?' He answered, 'You have said so.'" (Matthew 26: 14-30)

My Talk with Jesus

Judas' act of betrayal caused Jesus so much pain and sorrow that he wished the Son of Darkness had never been born. Still, deep down, Jesus knew that Judas had a role to play in God's plan of human salvation. Jesus was deeply hurt, because He had picked Judas to be one of the twelve apostles and had done so much with him. Yet, He could not change the heart of this betrayer and move him to the light. If someone has ever betrayed us, we would know how painful and heartbroken that experience is. Could we ever forgive and forget the one who betrayed us?

The first Biblical example of betrayal comes from the New Testament in the story of King Herod and the Three Wise Men. These men were lost in their search for Baby Jesus, the newborn King of the Jews. They came to King Herod to ask for help. The King felt threatened by the news of the birth of Jesus and decided to trick the Three Wise Men into giving him a report after they had a visit with the Baby. But, his real intention was to kill Baby Jesus, who might take over his throne someday. With the help of the Holy Spirit, the Three Wise Men realized the true intention of King Herod and decided to return home without giving him a report. King Herod felt betrayed and became angry to the point of ordering the massacre of all baby boys younger than three years old in his kingdom. That was a negative and bad reaction to a betrayal experience.

Another Biblical example of betrayal comes from the Old Testament story of Joseph and his brothers. Joseph was the favorite son in the Jacob's family and always trusted that his brothers would protect and care for him. Later, he found out that those brothers tried to hurt him and eventually sold him to an Egyptian merchant. Joseph certainly felt betrayed, but did not react badly like King Herod. Instead, he learned to forgive them and reached out to help them when they were hungry and in a desperate situation. This is a praiseworthy and positive reaction to a terrible betrayal experience.

Lord Jesus, I want to see

Jesus, My Faithful Friend and Great Protector, you knew how it feels to have someone betray you. Even though you were deeply hurt and heartbroken because of that terrible experience, you did not get even with the one who betrayed you or try to take it out on the whole world. Rather, you showed us how to forgive and depend on God's love and mercy to overcome any experience of betrayal. I will certainly run into that painful experience at some point in my life. Help me learn to deal with it with mercy and forgiveness like you did.

My Promise

This week I will see if someone has ever betrayed me. Then, with God's grace and prayer, I will learn to forgive and let go of that bad experience as I try to be kind and merciful toward the world around me. Thank you, Jesus, My Faithful Friend and Great Protector. I love you!

Topic of the Week: Denial

"... They lit a fire in the middle of the courtyard and sat around it, and Peter sat down with them. When a maid saw him seated in the light, she looked intently at him and said, 'This man too was with Him.' But, he denied saying, 'Woman, I do not know Him.' A short while later someone else saw him and said, 'You too are one of them'; but Peter answered, 'My friend, I am not.' About an hour later, still another insisted, 'Assuredly, this man too was with Him, for he also is a Galilean.' But Peter said, 'My friend, I do not know what you are talking about.' Just as he was saying this, the cock crowed; and the Lord turned and looked at Peter; and Peter remembered the word of the Lord, how He said to him, 'Before the cock crows today, you will deny me three times.' He went out and began to weep bitterly..." (Luke 22:54-65)

My Talk with Jesus

People often deny something because they do not want to admit the truth. They might have done something wrong, but they do not want to accept responsibility for it. As such, they strongly deny that they had anything to do with it. They are afraid of the consequences of their actions. That seems to be the case with Peter. Apparently, the authority arrested Jesus and falsely accused Him of all kinds of wrongful things, even though He was not guilty of any of them. All His works, as we might recall from the Gospels, were about doing good things and helping others. Now they were looking for Jesus' followers and hoping to imprison or kill them all as they did to their Master.

The first follower of Jesus that the authority identified was

Peter. They saw him huddle with some folks around the fire in the courtyard and began to accuse him of being a follower of Jesus. If I were Peter in that courtyard, would I have had the courage and commitment to Jesus to answer loudly: "Yes, I am one of His disciples"? Or, would I be so fearful and unfaithful to the Lord that I was willing to deny knowing Him like Peter did? Jesus must have been heartbroken to learn that Peter did deny being His disciple as He predicted that Peter would do that. After everything the Lord taught and did for him, Peter could not stand up for Jesus in a tough time. Imagine one of our best friends at a popular party did not say hello and simply ignored us. That would hurt us deeply. That is exactly how Jesus felt.

Lord Jesus, I want to see

Jesus, My Lord and Savior, you knew how it felt to be denied and rejected by your own disciple, even though you had done lots of wonderful things with him. At the moment you needed support and witnessing the most, everyone seemed to run away from you. After Judas sold you for thirty pieces of silver, no one wanted to stand up for you against the mob and false accusations. Everyone simply let you suffer alone or denied knowing you at all. That made you feel sad, hurt, and all alone.

Unfortunately, those feelings continue to happen to you these days, as we do not stand up for you against a world that is not friendly to God and religion. I reject you when I am ashamed to make the sign of the Cross and pray before eating in public. I deny knowing you when I do not stand up for my Christian faith and values. I abandon you when I let the mob bully someone or do not come to you in prayer daily. Help me change and try to acknowledge you every day, so that you will not deny me as one of your flock in the Kingdom of Heaven.

My Promise

This week I will acknowledge you, Jesus, as my Lord and best friend by volunteering to say a prayer before a family meal or doing something nice for someone in your name, even if the public might make fun of it. Thank you, Jesus, My Lord and Savior. I love you!

Topic of the Week: The Cross

"As they led Him [Jesus] away, they took hold of a certain Simon, a Cyrenian, who was coming in from the country; and after laying the Cross on him, they made him carry it behind Jesus...When they came to the place called the skull, they crucified Him, and the criminals there; one on His right, the other on His left. Then Jesus said, 'Father, forgive them, they know not what they do.' They divided His garments by casting lots. The people stood by and watched, the rulers meanwhile sneered at Him and said, 'He saved others, let Him save Himself if He is the chosen one, the Messiah of God.' Even the soldiers jeered at Him. As they approached to offer Him wine, they called out, 'If you are King of the Jews, save yourself.' Above Him there was an inscription that read, 'This is the King of the Jews.' Now one of the criminals hanging there reviled Jesus, saying, 'Are you not the Messiah? Save yourself and us.' The other, however, rebuking him, said in reply, 'Have you no fear of God, for you are subject to the same condemnation? And indeed, we have been condemned justly, for the sentence we received corresponds to our crimes, but this man has done nothing criminal.' Then he said, 'Jesus, remember me when you come into your Kingdom.' Jesus replied to him, 'Amen I say to you, today you will be with me in Paradise.'" (Luke 23: 26-43)

My Talk with Jesus

It must have been sad and scary for the early disciples to see their Lord being hung on the Cross with the criminals. The Romans, who occupied the land of the Israelites, used the Cross as the way to punish and teach the public a lesson about obeying rules. If someone did something wrong against the Romans' rules, they would punish the person by putting him/her in jail. But, the worst form of punishment was to nail the person on the Cross.

Each religion or nation has its own symbol. For example, a Crescent Moon and a Star represent Islam. The Star of David stands for the Jewish religion. Or, the fifty stars and thirteen stripes on our flag symbolize our country, the United States of America. For us as Christians, the Cross is our symbol, and it represents our faith. For some, it stands for death, suffering, sadness, and humiliation. For others, it is the symbol of new life, victory, hope, and promises. Whenever we enter a Christian church, facility, or home chances are we will find the Cross. The main reason for this is because the Cross wants to greet all its visitors with the love of Jesus and call on them to be open to love and the Christian way of life. The Cross of Jesus is also used to drive away evil spirits and the power of darkness.

Lord Jesus, I want to see

Jesus, Son of God and Savior of the World, you used your Cross as the way to save us and act as the bridge to connect us to the Kingdom of Heaven. Without it, we might still be stuck in sin and not have a chance to enter Heaven. Your Cross has also shown the love of God for us. Yet, I might not have spent enough time with it in prayer. Instead, I might sit too long in front of my computer playing games or talking with my friends on the phone for hours. Like our world, I might do anything to run away from the Cross or reject it when being asked to hold high the Cross for others to see its saving power. I need to be proud of and grateful to your Cross for what it has done for me.

My Promise

This week I will spend time in prayer in front of your Cross and think about what it did for me. I cannot imagine where I would end up after this life if it was not for your Cross. Thank you, Jesus, Son of God and Savior of the World. I love you!

Topic of the Week: Service

"... Jesus knew that His hour had come to pass from this world to the Father. He loved His own in the world and He loved them to the end... So, during supper, fully aware that the Father had put everything into His power and that He had come from God and was returning to God, Jesus rose from supper and took off His outer garments. He took a towel and tied it around His waist. Then He poured water into a basin and began to wash the disciples' feet and dry them with the towel around His waist. He came to Simon Peter, who said to Him, 'Master, are you going to wash my feet?' Jesus answered and said to him, 'What am I doing, you do not understand now; but you will understand later.' Peter said to Him, 'You will never wash my feet.' Jesus answered him, 'Unless I wash you, you will have no inheritance with me.' Simon Peter said to Him, 'Master, then not only my feet, by my hands and head as well.' ... Jesus said to them, 'Do you realize what I have done for you? ... If I, therefore, the master and teacher, have washed your feet, you ought to wash one another's feet. I have given you a model to follow, so that as I have done for you, you should also do for one another... If you understand this, blessed are you if you do it..." (John 13:1-20)

My Talk with Jesus

Peter, along with many early disciples, was caught by surprise when Jesus rolled up His sleeves and bowed down to wash their feet. His humble act of feet washing for His disciples shows us His love and concern for them. It also lets us know the importance of service in the eyes of Jesus. We cannot imagine that our Lord would bow down to wash the feet of His disciples. But Jesus did carry out this humble act. So, being a Christian means being people of service to one's neighbors.

In case you might not know, the Bible is full of examples of service. Abraham was called to lead God's people to the Promised Land, and he was more than willing to take on this responsibility. He wanted to serve God and God's people faithfully to the end of his life. Moses was another example of service, as we learn how God chose him to free God's people from slavery and lead them out of Egypt. He did not quit in the middle of it and abandon God's people in the desert. One more example of service comes from St. Paul in the New Testament. After he turned his life around, he was committed to put up with many hardships and travel all over the world to serve the needs of God's people.

Lord Jesus, I want to see

Jesus, the Faithful Servant of God and God's people, your whole life was about serving others: taking care of the sick, healing the lepers, driving out evil spirits from the possessed, feeding the hungry, and many other acts. Even on your last night on earth, you continued to serve God's people by washing your disciples' feet. I might think about myself all the time and find it difficult to worry about others, especially the poor and the misfortunate. The world might even influence me to be selfish, lazy, and less caring. It might look down on servants and make fun of people who bow down and wash the feet of others. But in your eyes, someone who dares to serve others makes you proud and helps bring God's love to the world. As a Christian, I am called to serve you, your Church, and everyone around me. I will be rewarded abundantly for all my services here on earth in your Kingdom.

My Promise

This week I will volunteer to help my family, friends, neighbors, or someone in need and take pride in serving others, especially the poor and the misfortunate. I will follow your great example of service. Thank you, Jesus, the Faithful Servant of God and God's people. I love you!

APRIL

Lord Jesus, I Want to See...

Topic of the Week: Hope

"On the first day of the week, Mary Magdalene came to the tomb early in the morning, while it was still dark, and saw the stone removed from the tomb. So, she ran and went to Simon Peter and the other disciple whom Jesus loved, and told them, 'They have taken the Lord from the tomb, and we do not know where they put Him.' So, Peter and the other disciple went out and came to the tomb. They both ran, but the other disciple ran faster than Peter and arrived at the tomb first; he bent down and saw the burial cloths there, but did not go in. When Simon Peter arrived after him, he went into the tomb and saw the burial cloths there, and the cloth that had covered His head, not with the burial cloths but rolled up in a separate place. Then, the other disciple also went in, the one who had arrived at the tomb first, and he saw and believed..." (John 20:1-10)

My Talk with Jesus

Every day we hear a lot about hope and its role in helping us stay alive. Without hope, we cannot survive another day or have the desire to keep on living. We learn that people who have faced difficult times like wars, losing a loved one, suffering bad health, breaking up with a friend, or having a bad time in school rely on hope to help them overcome bad past experiences and continue to live. These folks are usually heartbroken, lost, and overwhelmed. Without hope and help from God, they would never be able to last another day and find joy and desire for living. Hope and God's grace give them an energy boost and help them see the purpose for their living. Hope has unbelievable power; and if we are lucky enough to find it, we can experience life, peace, joy, and many wonderful blessings.

Apparently, that is what Mary Magdalene, Peter, and John experienced when they found some hope in an empty tomb. Everyone thought that it was the end of everything with the burial of Jesus. But to their surprise, they found an empty tomb when they went to mourn His death at His burial place. That event gave them hope and renewed their beliefs in Jesus and His mission of saving the world. They no longer felt depressed, hopeless, and fearful, but were filled with hope, excitement, and courage. They went out to tell the whole world about the risen Lord and the Easter miracle.

Lord Jesus, I want to see

Jesus, source of Life and Hope, you brought hope and new life to your disciples with the empty tomb and your resurrection when they were in pain, sorrow, and fear. Like your disciples, I have had moments of hopelessness and bad days. There have been times when I have felt overwhelmed by responsibilities, competition, expectations, and pressure in life. My family might have expected too much from me, and I do not know if I could live up to their big expectations. I do not want to disappoint them, but do not know what to do. Or, there might be all sorts of pressure and competition surrounding me every day. I sure do not want to be the least popular kid in the school or have no friends. I have felt overwhelmed, confused, and hopeless at times. But, I have seen what you did for the early disciples and God's people by giving them hope with your resurrection. I need to come to you often in prayer to receive the same blessing, especially when I feel lost, hopeless, and overwhelmed.

My Promise

This week I will examine deep down in my heart to see what might have made me feel hopeless or overwhelmed lately. Then, I will bring it to you, Jesus, in prayer to find an answer and some hope for it. Thank you, Jesus, source of Life and Hope. I love you!

Topic of the Week: Mercy

"… That is why the Kingdom of Heaven may be likened to a king who decided to settle accounts with his servants. When he began the accounting, a debtor was brought before him who owed him a huge amount. Since he had no way of paying it back, his master ordered him to be sold, along with his wife, his children, and all his property, in payment of the debt. At that, the servant fell down, did him homage, and said, 'Be patient with me, and I will pay you back in full.' Moved with compassion, the master of that servant let him go and forgave him the loan. When that servant had left, he found one of his fellow servants who owed him a much smaller amount. He seized him and started to choke him, demanding, 'Pay back what you owe.' Falling to his knees, his fellow servant begged him, 'Be patient with me, and I will pay you back.' But he refused. Instead, he had him put in prison until he paid back the debt. Now, when his fellow servants saw what had happened, they were deeply disturbed, and went to their master and reported the whole affair. His master summoned him and said to him, 'You wicked servant! I forgave you your entire debt because you begged me to. Should you not have had pity on your fellow servant, as I had pity on you?' Then in anger his master handed him over to the torturers until he should pay back the whole debt…" (Matthew 18:21-35)

My Talk with Jesus

It's difficult to believe what that servant did to the other fellow servant after he was granted mercy and forgiveness for his own debt! He was mean and horrible toward his fellow servant who owed him just a small debt compared to what he was forgiven. He choked him, treated him badly, and imprisoned him until he paid back everything despite his nonstop begging. Other servants saw his bad treatment of a fellow servant and were horrified by the whole thing. They reported it to the King, who quickly called for that merciless servant and yelled at him, "You wicked servant! I forgave you your entire debt because you begged me to. Should you not have had pity on your fellow servant, as I had pity on you?" Then in anger, the King demanded that the wicked servant pay back all his debt and handed him over to the guards who punished him severely.

We might think that the wicked and merciless servant was bad. But the truth is that we might do the same thing every day to our families, friends, and people around us. God has forgiven us time and time again for all the wrong things we have done. God has treated us kindly and mercifully because we have asked for it. God hopes we can do the same in dealing with others. Sadly, we might forget how God has treated us, and we treat others badly, such as not allowing our siblings to play with us or getting back at our friends for what bad things they do to us.

Lord Jesus, I want to see

Jesus, Kind and Merciful God, you do not just teach us about treating one another mercifully using stories like the one above. You also showed us by your own acts of compassion toward everyone around you, including your enemies. I still need lots of work and practice to have your attitude and act mercifully like you did. But with your help, I will commit myself to treat everyone mercifully and try to forgive others more often. I will learn to appreciate your mercy and forgiveness for me on the Cross and imitate your example.

My Promise

This week, I will think about some fight or argument that I had with my family, siblings, or friends. I will also recall how much you, Lord, have been merciful and forgiving to me. I will try to forgive and treat others mercifully. Thank you, Jesus, Kind and Merciful God. I love you!

Topic of the Week: Love

"... As the Father loves me, so I also love you. Remain in my love. If you keep my Commandments, you will remain in my love, just as I have kept my Father's Commandments and remain in His love. I have told you this so that my joy might be in you and your joy might be complete. This is my Commandment: Love one another as I love you. No one has greater love than this, to lay down one's life for one's friends. You are my friends if you do what I command you... This I command you: Love one another." (John 15:9-17)

My Talk with Jesus

As we know, God created us out of love. Then, after seeing the power of darkness try to lure us away from Heaven, God decided to save us out of love and sent God's only Son Jesus to sacrifice Himself on the Cross for us. Meanwhile, the Scripture passage says that God wants us to remain in God's love and continue to share it with the world around us. So, love seems to be an important thing that we should have in our lives always. It is like the air we breathe, the water we drink, or the sun we see on a beautiful day. If we do not have fresh air to breathe for a short moment, we end up dead. If we do not drink water daily, we will get dehydrated and eventually die. Or if we do not see the sun for days, we will feel sad, depressed, and grumpy. Like the sun, love makes us feel happy and excited. Like the air and water, love keeps us alive and gives us a desire to live.

We can see why God keeps filling our lives with love and calls us to live in love. The Bible is full of stories about love and how it helped God's people overcome their daily difficulties and survive over thousands of years. First, God saw how lonely and sad Adam was even though he had everything in the Garden of Eden. God gave him Eve to be his wife so that she could love him, and he would do the same for her. Their love eventually brought about a wonderful family of two children, Cain and Abel. Another great story in the Bible about love is how God gave us Jesus with His birth into the Holy Family. In this family, we see a lot of love and care for one another. Joseph, Jesus' foster father, worked hard as a carpenter to provide for the family, while Mary, His mother, took care of the family with love. We have also read in the Bible and seen in real life all the mean and bad things people do to one another when there is no love. Cain hurt Abel because he did not love his brother. God's people did not love Jesus and His disciples. They ended up crucifying Him on the Cross and hurting lots of Christians over the centuries. When people do not live in love, they do lots of hurtful things to others and create fights and wars all around them.

Lord Jesus, I want to see

Jesus, my Loving and Kind Friend, your whole life was about caring for others. Because of that attitude and spirit, you have filled our world with love, kindness, compassion, and good deeds. You have poured into our world of darkness with your Heavenly light. Everyone very much missed you when you returned to Heaven. I need to follow your example and commit myself to live a life of love. I must do more acts of love in my home, church, school, and neighborhood. I will try to avoid anything that is mean, hateful, and evil, for I want to create a world where everyone is kind, loving, and caring.

My Promise

This week I vow to avoid saying and doing anything that is mean and hurtful to people around me. Instead, I will do as many acts of love and kindness as I can for my family, my friends, and people around me. Thank you, Jesus, my Loving and Kind Friend. I love you!

Topic of the Week: Hate

"You have heard that it was said, 'You shall love your neighbor and hate your enemy. But I say to you, love your enemies, and pray for those who persecute you, that you may be children of your Heavenly Father, for He makes His Sun rise on the bad and the good, and causes rain to fall on the just and the unjust. For if you love those who love you, what recompense will you have? Do not tax collectors do the same? And if you greet your brothers/sisters only, what is unusual about that? Do not the pagans do the same? So, be perfect, just as your Heavenly Father is perfect." (Matthew 5:43-48)

My Talk with Jesus

The world usually tells us to love our neighbors and hate our enemies. That typical attitude is what we see around us every day, including hateful acts and angry talk reported on the news. On some occasions, students who did not like certain peers or teachers in their school decided to go there one day and shoot many innocent people. Their hatred pushed them to hurt not only folks they hate, but also many other innocents. We have seen terrorist groups like ISIS declare their hatred for the Christian faith, the USA, and Western culture. And then some of them go to some public places to shoot and blow up innocent people. We have also heard how people with different opinions become hateful and try to hurt one another.

Hatred is the feeling we might have toward someone we do not like. It usually brings about anger, fights, arguments, mean words, hurtful acts, and many, many evil deeds. The Bible gives us many examples about hatred, and it warns us to avoid it. For example, King Saul of the Israelites became jealous of David and plotted to hurt him after David's victory over the giant Philistine Goliath. He hated all the praises that the people gave to David. Another example is how other nations invaded Israel and made God's people their slaves. In return, the world called on God's people to hate those nations and take revenge on their people. But, God asks them to love and forgive, as they were blessed with a new life and a new country. Sadly, the world continues to base its justice system on this rule: "If you do bad things to me, I am going to do bad things back to you." Instead, we must replace hatred with the love of Jesus.

Lord Jesus, I want to see

Jesus, a Person of Love and Peace, you were different from other rabbis, prophets, and preachers. Your teachings have made that clear to me and the world as you call me to love my enemies and replace hatred with love. I know that when someone does something bad to me, I want to do the same thing back to that person. But, that simply continues that circle of hatred and vengeance. Give me courage and determination to be different from the world and follow your example by promoting love and peace instead of hatred and violence. By doing this, I will help change our world and make it a better place over time. The Prayer of St. Francis summarizes well my thinking: "Lord, make me an instrument of your peace: Where there is hatred, let me sow love; where there is injury, pardon; where there is doubt, faith; where there is despair, hope; where there is darkness, light; where there is sadness, joy..."

My Promise

This week, I will keep myself from saying any mean things or doing anything hateful and evil. I will say only kind things and do only loving and peaceful acts, even when someone makes me angry. Thank you, Jesus, a Person of Love and Peace. I love you!

MAY

Lord Jesus, I Want to See...

Topic of the Week: Counsel

"If you love me, you will keep my Commandments. And I will ask the Father, and He will give you another Advocate to be with you always, the Spirit of truth, which the world cannot accept; because it neither sees nor knows it. But you know it, because it remains with you, and will be in you. I will not leave you orphans; I will come to you. In a little while, the world will no longer see me; but you will see me because I live and you will live. On that day, you will realize that I am in my Father and you are in me and I in you. Whoever has my Commandments and observes them is the One who loves me. And whoever loves me will be loved by my Father, and I will love him/her and reveal myself to him/her... I have told you this while I am with you. The Advocate, the Holy Spirit that the Father will send in my name – He will teach you everything and remind you of all that I told you..." (John 14:15-31)

My Talk with Jesus

In stories and movies, the moment before someone dies is a very important time. The dying person usually mouths to his/her close friends and family members some wonderful counsel or important secret. The Scripture passage above wants to give us the same experience, as it shares with us the last words of Jesus before His return to Heaven. These last words should be considered a very important counsel and valuable treasure that our Lord left behind for His disciples. By following this great counsel, we will make it through this life safely and be reunited with Him some day in Heaven.

Important people like the President, kings and queens, and the Pope get counsel from a group of advisors daily. These advisors tell them what they should do and how they should make decisions. That way, they avoid doing wrong things or making bad decisions. But, they are not the only people who have great resources to help them in their lives and works. Students often come to their counselors in school to talk about their school work, troubles in their lives, plans, and other important issues. Smart students depend on their counselors or trusted adults like their parents, clergy, teachers, and coaches to give them wise counsel and good advice. That way they can avoid doing wrong things or making bad decisions.

Knowing the right people from whom to get wise counsel is very important. Many of us use the Internet these days to find all kinds of information. But, the Internet only gives information on certain things and does not bring us a happy life or tell us what to do when we have a bad day. Besides, the Internet and other untrustworthy sources might give us bad advice. As Christians, we must come to Jesus in prayer and ask Him for right counsel and comfort through all the good and bad moments in our lives.

Lord Jesus, I want to see

Jesus, My Teacher and Counselor, people came to you from all over during your ministry to hear your life-giving teaching and wise counsel. Even Nicodemus, a smart old religious leader, sought you out at night to get words of wisdom from you. I might or might not have someone to give me the right counsel yet. But from now on, I will count on you as my trustworthy counselor and come to you often in prayer for the best counsel. That way I will avoid doing wrong things and enjoy a good, joyful life every day.

My Promise

This week I will think about something for which I might need some counsel or guidance from Jesus, such as a problem with a certain school subject, teacher, classmate, sibling, or health issue. Then, I will come to you, Lord, in prayer and ask for help. Thank you, Jesus, my Teacher and Counselor. I love you!

Topic of the Week: Creation

"In the beginning, when God created the Heavens and the earth, the earth was a formless wasteland, and darkness covered the abyss, while a mighty wind swept over the waters. Then God said, 'Let there be light,' and there was light. God saw how good the light was. God then separated the light from the darkness. God called the light 'day', and the darkness God called 'night'. Thus, evening came and morning followed – the First day. Then God said, 'Let there be a dome in the middle of the waters, to separate one body of water from the other.' ...God called the dome 'the sky'. Evening came and morning followed – the Second day. Then God said, 'Let the water under the sky be gathered into a single basin, so that the dry land may appear.' ...God called the dry land 'the earth' and the basin of water 'the sea'. God saw how good it was. Then God said, 'Let the earth bring forth vegetation: every kind of plant that bears seed and every kind of fruit tree on earth that bears fruit with its seed in it.' And so it happened... Evening came and morning followed – the Third day. Then God said, 'Let there be lights in the dome of the sky, to separate day from night...' God made the two great lights, the greater one to govern the day, and the lesser one to govern the night; and God made the stars... God saw how good it was. Evening came and morning followed – the Fourth day. Then God said, 'Let the water team with abundance of living creatures, and on earth let birds fly beneath the dome of the sky.'...God blessed them... Evening came and morning followed – the Fifth day. Then God said, 'Let the earth bring forth all kinds of living creatures: cattle, creeping things, and wild animals of all kinds.'...Then God said: 'Let us make man in our image, after our likeness. Let them have dominion over the fish of the sea, the birds of the air, and the cattle, and over the wild animals and all the creatures that crawl on the ground.' ...God blessed them... And so it happened... Evening came and morning followed – the Sixth day. Thus, the Heavens and the earth and all their arrays were completed. Since on the Seventh day God was finished with the work God had been doing, God rested on the Seventh day and made it holy..." (Genesis 1-2)

My Talk with Jesus

We all know the story of Creation and how God created the Universe. We have heard about it so many times that we have forgotten how amazing God's work was. God put every little thing in the whole Universe together and got it to work in harmony without a glitch. Most spectacularly, God created the whole Universe out of nothing. So, we should give all the credit to God and thank God for giving us a wonderful world, especially for the gift of life. Unfortunately, people tend to destroy things rather than build or create things. We all should take good care of God's Creation.

Lord Jesus, I want to see

Jesus, Author of Life and King of the Universe, you were with God the Father at the moment of Creation and knew how special God's Creation was. You tried to save it by offering your own life on the Cross. I am living in a time when many people take the gift of life for granted and do not hesitate to destroy it if it does not fit neatly into their convenient, comfortable lifestyle. People do not realize how valuable the gift of life is. With your help, I will learn to appreciate the gift of life and preserve it at all costs. I will also try to build up

God's Creation and make it last for many centuries to come.

My Promise

This week, I will take time to thank you, Lord, for the gift of my life. I will also try to take care of God's Creation by planting a tree or preventing any trashing and destruction of the earth. Thank you, Jesus, Author of Life and King of the Universe. I love you!

Topic of the Week: Anger

"... When the Lord saw how great was human wickedness on the earth, and how no desire that His heart conceived was ever anything but evil, He regretted that He had made human beings on earth, and His heart was grieved. So the Lord said: 'I will wipe out from the earth the men whom I have created, and not only the men but also the beasts and the creeping things and the birds of the air, for I am sorry that I made them.' But, Noah found favor with the Lord... Noah, a good man and blameless in that age, for he walked with God, begot three sons: Shem, Ham, and Japheth. In the eyes of God, the earth was corrupt and full of lawlessness. When God saw how corrupt the earth had become, since all mortals led depraved lives on earth, He said to Noah: 'I have decided to put an end to all mortals on earth; the earth is full of lawlessness because of them. So I will destroy them and all life on earth... I, on my part, am about to bring the flood on the earth, to destroy everywhere all creatures in which there is the breadth of life; everything on earth shall perish. But with you [Noah], I will establish my covenant; you and your sons, your wife and your sons' wives, shall go into the ark. Of all other living creatures you shall bring two into the ark, one male and one female, that you may keep them alive with you... This Noah did; he carried out all the Commands that God gave him... For forty days and forty nights, heavy rain poured down on the earth... The waters maintained their crest over the earth for one hundred and fifty days, and then God remembered Noah and all the animals, wild and tame, that were with him in the ark. So, God made a wind sweep over the earth, and the waters began to subside... Gradually the waters receded from the earth... Noah lived three hundred and fifty years after the flood." (Gen 6-9)

My Talk with Jesus

We have heard a lot about God's wrath, but the Scripture passage above is one of the few examples that shows it and its consequences. After God worked hard to create an amazing Creation, God's people disobeyed God's Commands and slowly turned toward evil and darkness. God became angry and decided to wipe them all out and start anew. But, God let Noah know about the epic flood and told him to build an ark to prepare for it. His family and all kinds of God's Creatures were saved as they took shelter in the ark. Anger is certainly a powerful emotion that can cause great damage such as destroying families and property, causing people to make wrong decisions, and so on. Because of its bad effects in our lives, anger has been listed as one of the seven deadly sins. We are called to avoid it.

Lord Jesus, I want to see

Jesus, source of Peace and Kindness, you could have turned angry and gotten into all kinds of arguments with religious leaders because they kept bullying and harassing you. But, you got your anger under control and tried to find peaceful ways to resolve your differences. Sometimes my family, siblings, and friends might make me mad, and I want to scream bad things to their face and do mean things to them. But with your help and example, I will try to be a person of peace and walk away from those moments of anger. I will look for other ways to deal with differences between me and others around me. Moreover, I will promote peace and help others choose that way to deal with the problems in their lives.

My Promise

This week I will try not to get angry with my family, my friends, or people around me. If I am getting provoked or find something bothering me, I will choose a peaceful way to deal with that problem. Thank you, Jesus, source of Peace and Kindness. I love you!

Topic of the Week: Generosity

"The Kingdom of Heaven is like a landowner who went out at dawn to hire laborers for his vineyard. After agreeing with them for the usual daily wage, he sent them into his vineyard. Going out about nine o'clock, he saw others standing idle in the market place, and he said to them, 'You too go into vineyard, and I will give you what is just. So, they went off. And he went out again around noon, and around three o'clock, and did likewise. Going out about five o'clock, he found others standing around, and said to them, 'Why do you stand here idle all day?' They answered, 'Because no one has hired us.' He said to them, 'You too go into my vineyard.' When it was evening, the owner of the vineyard said to his foreman, 'Summon the laborers and give them their pay, beginning with the last and ending with the first.' When those who had started about five o'clock came, each received the usual daily wage. So, when the first came, they thought that they would receive more, but each of them also got the usual wage. And on receiving it they grumbled against the landowner, saying, 'These last ones worked only one hour; and you have made them equal to us, who bore the day's burden and the heat.' He said to one of them in reply, 'My friend, I am not cheating you. Did you not agree with me for the usual daily wage? Take what is yours and go. What if I wish to give this last one the same as you? Am I not free to do as I wish with my own money? Are you envious because I am generous?' Thus, the last will be first, and the first will be last." (Matthew 20:1-16)

My Talk with Jesus

Like God the Father, the landowner invited people to work for his vineyard at different times throughout the day and agreed to pay a just wage for each of them when they were hired. At the end of the day, he gathered all his workers to give them their pay. He decided to give the workers who were hired last the same pay as the ones who were hired first. Instead of being happy for the last ones, the first workers became jealous. They basically did not want the last workers to receive the same pay as they did despite the generous nature of the landowner. This story tells us a lot about God and humanity. God is always generous, whereas we humans are quite stingy and selfish with one another.

None of us was born with a generous nature. We tend to be selfish and do not want to share. We might see someone in need of help; but somehow, we do not try to reach out and give that person some assistance. Our world is surely full of rich people. Sadly, it still has a lot of people who go hungry every day or sleep underneath the highway. Many children must go to God's kitchen right after school to find a meal. Since people are not generous in sharing God's blessings for them with others.

Lord Jesus, I want to see

Jesus, Generous and Caring God, you once praised the poor widow who donated only two cents to the Temple. Many rich people donated more than she did. But in your eyes, she gave more than all the rich people, because she gave everything she had, whereas the rich did it out of their own surplus. I might get stuck with the same virus of "selfish and greedy" like the world does. But with your help, I will try to be generous and learn to share God's blessings for me with my siblings, my friends, and misfortunate people around me. That way, I will be rewarded abundantly in your Kingdom someday.

My Promise

This week I will see what my family, friends, and neighbors might need. Then, I will gladly volunteer my time to help and generously share with them what I have. This act of generosity will make me feel good and you, Lord, will be proud of me. Thank you, Jesus, Generous and Caring God. I love you!

JUNE

Lord Jesus,
I Want to See...

Topic of the Week: Disobedience

"Now the serpent was the most cunning of all the animals that the Lord God had made. The serpent asked the woman, 'Did God really tell you not to eat from any of the trees in the garden?' The woman answered the serpent: 'We may eat of the fruit of the trees in the garden; it is only about the fruit of the tree in the middle of the garden that God said, 'You shall not eat it or even touch it; lest you die.'' But the serpent said to the woman: 'You certainly will not die! No, God knows well that the moment you eat of it your eyes will be opened and you will be like gods who know what is good and what is bad.' The woman saw that the tree was good for food, pleasing to the eyes, and desirable for gaining wisdom. So she took some of its fruit and ate it; and she also gave some to her husband, who was with her, and he ate it. Then, the eyes of both of them were opened, and they realized that they were naked; so they sewed fig leaves together and made loincloths for themselves... Then the Lord said to the serpent: 'Because you have done this, you shall be banned from all the animals and from all the wild creatures; on your belly you shall crawl, and dirt shall you eat all the days of your life... To the woman He said: 'I will intensify the pangs of your childbearing; in pain shall you bring forth children. Yet, your urge shall be for your husband, and he shall be your master.' To the man He said: 'Because you listened to your wife and ate from the tree of which I had forbidden you to eat; cursed be the ground because of you! In toil shall you eat its yield all the days of your life. Thorns and thistles shall it bring forth to you... By the sweat of your face shall you get bread to eat, until you return to the ground ...'" (Genesis 3:1-24)

My Talk with Jesus

Obedience is one of the virtues we all find difficult to practice in our daily lives. We all want to do things our own way, and do not want to listen to anyone or follow any rules. In the Bible story above, the Devil takes on the form of a serpent and tries to convince Eve and Adam to listen to no one and eat the forbidden fruit. It makes them believe that the only reason God forbade them to eat the fruit in the middle of the Garden was because God did not want them to become like gods. So, the couple trusted the serpent and disobeyed God by eating the forbidden fruit.

We live in a time that does not respect God. Everyone does whatever they want and often disobeys God's Commandments. Anyone can shoot and hurt others without fearing God's wrath and punishment. People cheat and steal without worrying that God will make them repay it on the Day of Judgment. Unless our world turns its life around and stops disobeying God, there will be all kinds of evil things and violence around us every day.

Lord Jesus, I want to see

Jesus, Judge of the Living and the Dead; you are very compassionate and understanding to sinners who come to you and ask for forgiveness. But, you are also very clear in telling people to stop disobeying God and turn their lives back to God. I have violated certain rules and disobeyed my parents, and that disappoints them. I have not listened to people in authority and have done things contrary to what I'm supposed to do. My wrong actions have shown my lack of respect and love for God and others. With your help, I will learn to listen, obey, and respect people in authority. I will act contrary to what the Devil and the world want me to do.

My Promise

This week I will try to do what my parents, teachers, coaches, clergy, catechists, or people of authority ask of me, even though it might be difficult. I will also learn not to talk back so that I show respect and obedience to God and others. Thank you, Jesus, Judge of the Living and the Dead. I love you!

Topic of the Week: Fighting

"The mother of the sons of Zebedee approached Him [Jesus] with her sons and did Him homage, wishing to ask Him for something. He said to her, 'What do you wish?' She answered Him, 'Command that these two sons of mine sit, one at your right and the other at your left, in your Kingdom.' Jesus said in reply, 'You do not know what you are asking. Can you drink the cup that I am going to drink?' They said to Him, 'We can.' He replied, 'My cup you will indeed drink, but to sit at my right and at my left, this is not mine to give but is for those for whom it has been prepared by my Father.' When the ten heard this, they became indignant at the two brothers. But Jesus summoned them and said, 'You know that the rulers of the Gentiles lord it over them, and the great ones make their authority over them felt. But it shall not be so among you. Rather, whoever wishes to be great among you shall be your servant; whoever wishes to be first among you shall be your slave..." (Matthew 20:20-28)

My Talk with Jesus

We might think that the apostles and early disciples did not fight. But, the truth is that they fought about almost everything. The Gospel passage above shares one of those fights among the apostles. This fight came about because the mother of the sons of Zebedee asked Jesus to let her sons sit on both sides of Him in God's Kingdom. The other disciples overheard it and started to fight with the two brothers. They probably told the two brothers, "Who do you think you are? We have been following the Lord long before you two even showed up. All of a sudden you jump in and want to have the best seats in God's

Kingdom? Get in line, buddies!" Certainly, we can picture the Apostles pushing and shoving each other while exchanging words of insult and taunting.

That is how most fights begin. People have their differences about something, and then begin to quarrel. One side states one's opinion about the problem at hand and why they think their opinion is right. Meanwhile, the other side voices their own arguments as to why they are also right and the rest are simply wrong. The heated exchange of two sides goes from name calling and insults to fist fights and other forms of physical violence. This whole circle of fighting can go on for a long time and that could affect everyone. No one talks to each other or desires to create a peaceful world. And, this is exactly what the Devil wants our world to be, hating one another and being far away from God's love.

Lord Jesus, I want to see

Jesus, source of Peace and Love, you saw how fighting and hatred turned the Israelites against the Romans, who were their occupiers and mistreated them badly. God's people were hoping that you would become their political Messiah and lead them in a fight against the Romans. But, you did not step in because you have seen only bad things come out of a fight. That is why you always tried to stop a fight before it became out of control. As we see in the Gospel passage above, you stopped the disciples from fighting with one another and called them to be servants. I might get into fights often with people around me, especially when being provoked by my siblings or schoolmates. With your help and example, I will do everything possible to avoid fights and help others stop fighting. Fighting only brings hurt, pain, tears, sadness, and other damages.

My Promise

This week I will try to avoid any fighting with my family, my friends, and others around me. If I am currently fighting with someone, I will come to you, Lord, in prayer and ask you to help me make peace and reconcile with that person. Thank you, Jesus, source of Peace and Love. I love you!

Topic of the Week: Calmness

"On that day, as evening drew on, He [Jesus] said to them, 'Let us cross to the other side.' Leaving the crowd, they took Him with them in the boat just as He was. And the other boats were with Him. A violent storm came up and waves were breaking over the boat, so that it was already filling up. Jesus was in the stern, asleep on a cushion. They woke Him and said to Him, 'Teacher, do you not care that we are perishing?' He woke up, rebuked the wind, and said to the sea, 'Quiet, be still!' The wind ceased and there was a great calm. Then, He asked them, 'Why are you terrified? Do you not yet have faith?' They were filled with great awe and said to one another, 'Who then is this whom even wind and sea obey?' (Mark 4:35-41)

My Talk with Jesus

No one wants to be caught in the middle of the storm. The heavy, violent wind scares us! Then, there is lightning and thunder, which makes us jump. Also, heavy rain can keep coming down from Heaven like a waterfall. If we have been caught in a storm ourselves, we know how scary this can be. Some of the disciples apparently were with Jesus in the boat when they ran into a bad storm. The big waves and strong wind threatened to sink the boat and put their lives in danger. The disciples had to call on Jesus to calm the storm and bring serenity to their lives.

Like the disciples, we want our lives to be calm, serene, peaceful, and happy. We want everything to run smoothly and go our way every day. But, the truth is that many things go wrong in our lives. Our siblings can sometimes be a constant annoyance and get us into lots of fights. Our friends can harass us and get us into trouble at school. Our teachers can be mean and make our school days quite long. Our pets or loved ones might die and make us feel sad. Our life difficulties can make us feel scared and worried.

Lord Jesus, I want to see

Jesus, my Help and Protection, you came to the rescue for your disciples on a stormy night. You calmed the wind, silenced the storm, and restored their lives to normal. You also helped bring peace and joy to many homes during your ministry. I might feel scared and not know where to go to ask for help when something unpleasant has happened in my life. But, after hearing the story above on how the disciples came to ask you to rescue them from a violent storm, I know I should come to you whenever I need help or feel scared about something. If, for some reason, I feel that you did not hear me, I need to call louder and be persistent with my prayer request, just like your disciples did.

I want a calm, peaceful, and happy life. But, sometimes I might create a stormy and horrified living situation for my family and people around me. When things do not go my way, I might throw a tantrum, scream at others, and act violently toward people who I believe are responsible for my plight. When I ignore or refuse to do what I was asked, I basically create a storm that might scare and worry people around me. I need to stop bringing violent storms into my home, school, and church. I need to imitate your example and learn to bring calmness and peace to others, instead of storms.

My Promise

This week, I will try to speak gently, act calmly, and keep a peaceful household even when others might harass or provoke me and make me mad. I will also come to you, Lord, in prayer to ask for help if I feel a storm in my life is getting out of control. Thank you, Jesus, my Help and Protection. I love you!

Topic of the Week: Goodness

"But because he [a scholar of the law] wished to justify himself, he said to Jesus, 'And who is my neighbor?' Jesus replied, 'A man fell victim to robbers as he went down from Jerusalem to Jericho. They stripped and beat him and went off leaving him half-dead. A Priest happened to be going down that road; but when he saw him, he passed by on the opposite side. Likewise, a Levite came to the place, and when he saw him, he passed by on the opposite side. But, a Samaritan traveler who came upon him was moved with compassion at the sight. He approached the victim, poured oil and wine over his wounds and bandaged them. Then he lifted him up on his own animal, took him to an inn and cared for him. The next day he took out two silver coins and gave them to the innkeeper with the instruction, 'Take care of him. If you spend more than what I have given you, I shall repay you on my way back.' Which of these three, in your opinion, was neighbor to the robbers' victim?' He answered, 'The one who treated him with mercy.' Jesus said to him, 'Go and do likewise.'" (Luke 10:29-37)

My Talk with Jesus

The story above is often known as the Good Samaritan Parable. It tells us about a man who travelled from Jerusalem to Jericho on a very dangerous journey with lots of gang activities and robbery. Unfortunately, the victim traveled this bad road alone and was robbed. His robbers not only took all his possessions but also beat him up badly and left him half dead in a ditch alongside the road. Two religious leaders—a Priest and a Levite—happened to pass by the same road and saw this poor victim in the ditch. But, they did not reach out and help this man. Perhaps they were in a hurry or did not want to get involved with the whole mess. Their actions were not good or commendable.

Thankfully, a Samaritan took that same road and came upon this poor victim in terrible shape. But, unlike the other two travelers, this one did not ignore the victim and leave him suffer. Instead, he jumped into the ditch, bandaged up the man, and took him to a nearby inn for further care. He also took out his own money to pay for all the costs of caring for this stranger. This Samaritan was taught in his culture not to do anything for a Jew. But, that did not stop him from doing a good deed and showing God's love to this Jewish victim. What this means is that doing good things for others has no limit or boundary. Everyone is called to practice the duty of goodness daily.

Lord Jesus, I want to see

Jesus, Good and Compassionate God, you spent your whole life doing good for others. You healed the sick, gave sight to the blind, drove out demons, fed the hungry, and restored life to the dead and the hopeless. You wanted to use the power of good to defeat evil and bring people closer to God, the source of goodness. I live in a time that does not encourage people to do more good things for others. Rather, the world emphasizes simply focusing on "me" and caring for my own needs. Worse yet, this creates many evil things and fosters hatred. But, that is not a healthy ground for good things to grow. I might not want to do good things all the time or stand up for something good. But with your help and encouragement, I will follow your example and do more good things for others. I will not be afraid to be the only one like you or the Good Samaritan who reached out and helped someone in need.

My Promise

This week I will try to do as many good deeds as possible. I will also not hesitate to stand up for something good or someone in need of help despite being mocked for doing that. Thank you, Jesus, Good and Compassionate God. I love you!

JULY

Lord Jesus, I Want to See...

Topic of the Week: Bravery

"... Laban and his household said in reply: 'This thing comes from the Lord; we can say nothing to you either for or against it. Here is Rebekah, ready for you, take her with you that she may become the wife of your master's son, as the Lord has said.' When Abraham's servant heard their answer, he bowed to the ground before the Lord. Then he brought out objects of silver and gold and articles of clothing and presented them to Rebekah; he also gave costly presents to her brother and mother... When they were up the next morning, he said, 'Let me leave to return to my master [Abraham].' Her brother and mother replied, 'Let the girl stay with us a short while, say ten days; after that she may go.' But he said to them, 'Do not detain me now that the Lord has made my errand successful; let me go back to my master.' They answered, 'Let us call the girl and see what she herself has to say about it.' So they called Rebekah and asked her, 'Do you wish to go with this man?' She answered, 'I do.' At this they allowed their sister Rebekah and her nurse to take leave, along with Abraham's servant and his men... Then Rebekah and her maids started out; they mounted their camels and followed the man... The servant recounted to Isaac all the things he had done. Then Isaac took Rebekah into his tent; he married her, and thus she became his wife..." (Genesis 24)

My Talk with Jesus

This week's Bible passage tells us the story of how Rebekah was chosen to be the bride for Isaac who was a stranger to her. She tried to honor her family and trusted that the Lord would guide her and watch over her. So, she accepted being

Isaac's wife and left her own family to create a family with him. Rebekah must have been quite brave and humble to do that. Maybe she was a bit scared because this was the first time she left her family and was on her own. Do anyone of us remember the first time we went away to a place on our own, like a summer camp? A brave person like Rebekah would not let any fear or difficulty keep her from doing the right thing.

Bravery or courage is one of the important virtues in our Christian faith. This virtue helped the early disciples go out to the world and preach the Good News after their Master was arrested and crucified on the Cross. They all were fearful for their lives after what the authorities did to Jesus. They could have been arrested and could have lost their lives. With the help of the Holy Spirit, they were filled with courage and no longer feared the authority or losing their lives. That is what bravery can do for a person and much more. It can help a person overcome any fear or worry.

Lord Jesus, I want to see

Jesus, My Brave Friend and Hero, you were brave enough to leave your comfortable home in Heaven and enter our world to preach your Good News and offer your own life on the Cross to save us. I am not sure if I am brave enough to deal with the world and many scary things in life. I am concerned that I might disappoint my family by doing poorly in school or that I might not have any friends or that my classmates will not include me in their games and activities. I am worried that I might not get good grades, even though I have worked hard in school. With your help and encouragement, I will come to you whenever I feel scared or worried. I will try to act bravely and reach out to do more good things for others, even though I might feel uneasy at times.

My Promise

This week I will think about something that might make me feel uncomfortable, worried, or scared. Then, I will bring it to you, Lord, in prayer and bravely deal with this problem head on. Thank you, Jesus, My Brave Friend and Hero. I love you!

Topic of the Week: Trials

"Having set out from Elim, the whole Israelite community came into the desert of sin, which is between Elim and Sinai, on the fifteenth day of the second month after their departure from the land of Egypt. Here in the desert the whole Israelite community grumbled against Moses and Aaron. The Israelites said to them, 'Would that we had died at the Lord's hand in the land of Egypt, as we sat by our fleshpots and ate our fill of bread? But you had to lead us into the desert to make the whole community die of famine!' Then the Lord said to Moses, 'I will now rain down bread from Heaven for you. Each day the people are to go out and gather their daily portion; thus will I test them, to see whether they follow my instructions or not... From the desert of sin the whole Israelite community journeyed by stages, as the Lord directed, and encamped at Rephidim. Here there was no water for the people to drink. They quarreled, therefore, with Moses and he said, 'Why do you quarrel with me? Why do you put the Lord to the test?' Here, then, in their thirst for water, the people grumbled against Moses, saying, 'Why did you ever make us leave Egypt? Was it just to have us die here of thirst with our children and our livestock?' ... The Lord answered Moses, '... I will be standing there in front of you on the rock in Horeb. Strike the rock, and the water will flow from it for the people to drink.' ... The place was called Massah and Meribah, because the Israelites quarreled there and tested the Lord, saying, 'Is the Lord in our midst or not?'..." (Exodus 16-17)

My Talk with Jesus

Today's Scripture passage tells us about a time when God's people were tested as they spent forty years in the desert on their way to the Promised Land. If you have ever been in the desert, you must admit that it is a very tough and hostile place to live. It is very hot during the day, while at night it gets very cold. Worst yet, it is very difficult to find water and food in the desert. But, without water and food, we humans die. Besides, there are all kinds of dangerous things in the desert that could harm a person.

Like God's people, our lives are constantly trialed. We might have to face some health problems. School might not come easily for us, and we struggle to deal with school work. Our families might have to go through a divorce separation or financial difficulty. We might have a problem making friends. For us as Christians, all the difficult things in our lives are part of the trials that we humans go through to prepare us for the Promised Land or Heaven. We rely on God to give us strength and courage to help us through these trials.

Lord Jesus, I want to see

Jesus, My Help and Guidance, your life was full of difficulties and suffering. You also witnessed many people whose lives were on trial because of health, lack of food, or feeling lost in this world. You reached out to give them a hand and called on them to have faith in you during those tough moments. I have been through some trials, and they have tested my strength, patience, resilience, and relationship with you. I call on you for help in prayer through these trials and not to lose faith in you when things do not turn out my way. I also need to know that these trial moments will make me a stronger and more compassionate person.

My Promise

This week I will review my life to see if I have dealt with any difficulties or trials lately. Then, I will ask you, Lord, in prayer to guide me through these times and simply trust you. Thank you, Jesus, My Help and Guidance. I love you!

Topic of the Week: Lost

"The tax collectors and sinners were all drawing near to listen to Him [Jesus], but the Pharisees and Scribes began to complain, saying, 'This man welcomes sinners and eats with them.' So, to them He addressed this parable. 'What person among you having a hundred sheep and losing one of them would not leave the ninety-nine in the desert and go after the lost one until he finds it? And when he does find it, he sets it on the shoulders with great joy and, upon his arrival home, he calls together his friends and neighbors and says to them, 'Rejoice with me because I have found my lost sheep. I tell you, in just the same way there will be more joy in Heaven over one sinner who repents than over ninety-nine righteous people who have no need of repentance." (Luke 15:1-7)

My Talk with Jesus

The Bible passage tells us about the classic story of the Good Shepherd and the lost sheep. The lost sheep likely felt scared, alone, hungry, and thirsty. For some reason, it wandered off from the fold and could not find its way home. It desperately needed help and frantically cried out to its shepherd to come and rescue it. If you have ever gone on a camping trip and ended up lost, you know exactly how the lost sheep felt. It is frightening to be lost and not know where we are. We cannot find our way home, and it is getting dark quickly. We might run into lots of dangerous and scary things while being lost in the middle of nowhere. We are all alone, scared, frustrated, exhausted, confused, hungry, and thirsty. We wonder if someone will come to rescue us while trying to search our way out. Being lost is certainly a terrifying feeling, and we cannot wait to be found.

Maybe you are lost at school. In school, there might be a subject or class that is hard to understand. You might not do well with tests or homework and get bad grades. If this happens, you might soon fall behind in class, end up feeling lost, and no longer want to come to school. You need help and want someone to rescue you from that horrible feeling. That help might come from a caring counselor or a dedicated teacher who patiently explains that difficult subject until you get it or find ways to get you to like the class and school.

Unfortunately, it is much more difficult to get help and find rescue when we feel lost in real life. There is no life expert or special counselor who can help us and guarantee a successful rescue. There are so many things in life that might overwhelm and scare us. We also do not want to disappoint our families and friends by not living up to their expectations. All those conflicting feelings might make us feel lost and frustrated about our life. But, we as Christians can come to Jesus and ask Him to rescue us from our life problems.

Lord Jesus, I want to see

Jesus, My Help and Guide, you once said, "I am the way, the truth, and the life" when Thomas told you that he did not know where you were going, and he could not find the way to Heaven. Like Thomas, I might feel lost in this life and not know how to get to Heaven. But with your guidance and support, I will be able to deal with all the difficulties in my life and find my way to Heaven. I will also learn how to handle daily pressure from society and friends and the expectations of my loved ones.

My Promise

This week I will think about something that makes me feel lost and worried. Then, I will ask you, Lord, in prayer to give me guidance and peace for that problem. With your helping hands, I will not feel lost. Thank you, Jesus, My Help and Guide. I love you!

Topic of the Week: Hospitality

"... After some time, however, the brook ran dry, because no rain had fallen in the land. So, the Lord said to him [Elijah]: 'Move on to Zarephath. As he arrived at the entrance of the city, a widow was gathering sticks there; he called out to her, 'Please bring me a small cupful water to drink.' She left to get it, and he called out after her, 'Please bring along also a bit of bread.' 'As the Lord, your God lives,' she answered, 'I have nothing baked; there is only a handful of flour in my jar and a little oil in my jug. Just now I was collecting a couple of sticks, to go in and prepare something for myself and my son; when we have eaten, we shall die.' 'Do not be afraid,' Elijah said to her. 'Go and do as you propose. But first make me a little cake and bring it to me. Then you can prepare something for yourself and your son. For the Lord, the God of Israel says, 'The jar of flour shall not go empty, nor the jug of oil run dry, until the day when the Lord sends rain upon the earth.' She left and did as Elijah had said. She was able to eat for a year, and he and her son as well; the jar of flour did not go empty, nor the jug of oil run dry, as the Lord had foretold through Elijah..." (1 Kings 17)

My Talk with Jesus

In some cultures, people show warm hospitality to their guests by giving them lots of good food. They are certainly not worried about the costs of food and hospitality, for they simply want to be good hosts to their guests. That seems to be the case in the story above. After a long journey, Prophet Elijah was hungry and thirsty. He decided to stop by the house of a widow in town to ask for something to eat and drink before continuing with his trip. What Elijah probably did not know was that the whole town had gone through a very bad drought, and its people could not grow anything. The result was a bad harvest and lack of food.

That was exactly what the poor widow and her only son had to face. She did not have much left to eat and was about to face starvation. That was certainly not the news Elijah or any visitor would want to hear from one's host. If the host had to face that desperate situation, a guest like Elijah might not get anything to eat. Fortunately, like many poor folks, this widow had a heart of gold and a generous spirit. She decided to share what little resources she had left with a stranger like Elijah. Like a good host, she could not let her guest go hungry. In return, Elijah asked the Lord to perform a miracle for the poor widow and her son for their hospitable and generous spirit.

Lord Jesus, I want to see

Jesus, Generous and Welcoming Host, while your disciples could not see the importance of good hospitality and wanted to turn away a hungry crowd to care for their own needs, you told them to take care of the needs of the crowd. You reached out and performed the miracle that multiplied the loaves and fish yourself. Your miracle and hospitality took care of several thousand hungry mouths that day. I might be influenced by our selfish culture and care very little about the community around me. I might not want to share God's blessings for me with others and may not try to be a good and welcoming host to my guests. But with your example, I will learn to show good hospitality and a generous spirit to all my guests, especially the unfortunate. Kindness and generosity will always be repaid.

My Promise

This week I will try to be a good host to my friends or anyone who happens to stop by my home. I will be welcoming and hospitable to all my guests without worrying about the costs. Thank you, Jesus, Generous and Welcoming Host. I love you!

AUGUST

Lord Jesus, I Want to See...

Topic of the Week: Daring

"Long afterward, in the third year, the Lord spoke to Elijah. 'Go present yourself to Ahab,' Obadiah went to meet Ahab and informed him. Ahab came to meet Elijah and when he saw Elijah, said to him, 'Is it you, you disturber of Israel?' 'It is not I who disturbs Israel,' he answered, 'but you and your family, by forsaking the commands of the Lord and following the Baal. Now summon all Israel to me on Mount Carmel, as well as the four hundred and fifty prophets of Asherah who eat at Jezebel's table.'... Then Elijah said to the people, 'I am the only surviving prophet of the Lord, and there are four hundred and fifty prophets of Baal. Give us two young bulls. Let them choose one, cut it into pieces, and place it on the wood, but start no fire. I shall prepare the other and place it on the wood, but shall start no fire. You shall call on your gods, and I will call on the Lord. The God who answers with fire is God.' All the people answered, 'Agreed!' ... Taking the young bull that was turned over to them, they prepared it and called on Baal from morning to noon, saying, 'Answer us, Baal!' But there was no sound, and no one answering... Noon passed and they remained in a prophetic state until the time for offering sacrifice. But there was not a sound; no one answered, and no one was listening... At the time for offering sacrifice, the prophet Elijah came forward and said, 'Lord, God of Abraham, Isaac, and Israel, let it be known this day that you are God in Israel and that I am your servant and have done these things by your command. Answer me, Lord! ...' The Lord's fire came down and consumed the holocaust, wood, stones, and dust, and it lapped up the water in the trench. Seeing this, all the people fell prostrate... Elijah then said to Ahab, 'Go up, eat and drink, for there is the sound of a heavy rain.' ... In a trice, the sky grew dark with clouds and wind, and a heavy rain fell..." (1Kings 18)

My Talk with Jesus

It is extremely difficult for us to find someone like the Prophet Elijah in our day and age. He stood up for his faith and did not let any idol worshiper like Baal followers make fun of his faith. He challenged Obadiah and Ahab—Baal worshipers—to a contest to see if their god or the God of the Israelites would come and accept the offering by sending fire from Heaven to burn it. But, after waiting for a long time and repeating their prayer to the god Baal, they got nothing. Then, Elijah called on the God of Abraham, Isaac, and Israel to hear his prayer, accept his offering, and send down fire from Heaven to burn it. That was exactly what happened.

Like many people back then, some Christians might run after other gods and forget about their loving God. Worse yet, they might not have courage to stand up to other people who might make fun of their faith. We must imitate the example of Elijah and dare those people to a contest, because our faithful God will always be there to answer our prayers.

Lord Jesus, I want to see

Jesus, My Faithful and Loving God, you always stand up to defend God the Father and give praise and thanks to Him every chance possible. Often, I let the world tell me what to believe. Or, sometimes, I am ashamed of my Christian faith and let others make fun of it and my beliefs. But with your grace and support, I will work on my relationship with you and try to grow closer to you. I should also stand up for my Christian faith at school and defend you without any hesitation.

My Promise

This week I will seek opportunities to defend my Christian faith and dare anyone to challenge my God. I will not be ashamed of my Christian faith by making the Cross before eating in public. I will strengthen my relationship with you through prayer. Thank you, Jesus, My Faithful and Loving God. I love you!

Topic of the Week: Jealousy

"... When Joseph was seventeen years old, he was tending the flocks with his brother... Jacob their father loved Joseph best of all his sons, for he was the child of his old age; and he had made him a long tunic. When his brothers saw that their father loved him best of all his sons; they hated him so much that they would not even greet him... One day, when his brothers had gone to pasture their father's flocks at Shechem, Jacob said to Joseph, 'Your brothers, you know, are tending our flocks at Shechem. Get ready; I will send you to them.' ... So Joseph went after his brothers and caught up with them in Dothan. They noticed him from a distance, and before he came up to them, they plotted to kill him... When Reuben heard this, he tried to save him from their hands, saying, 'We must not take his life. Instead of shedding his blood,' he continued, 'just throw him into that cistern there in the desert; but don't kill him outright.' ... So, when Joseph came up to them, they stripped him of the long tunic he had on; then they took him and threw him into the cistern, which was empty and dry... They saw a caravan of Ismaelites coming from Gilead, their camels laden with gum, balm, and resin to be taken down to Egypt... They sold Joseph to the Ismaelites for twenty pieces of silver. Some Midianite traders passed by, and they pulled Joseph up out of the cistern and took him to Egypt... The Midianites, meanwhile, sold Joseph in Egypt to Potiphar, a courtier of Pharaoh and his chief Steward." (Genesis 37)

My Talk with Jesus

The Bible is full of stories about jealousy. For example, when Cain saw how God seemed to favor his younger brother, Abel, over him, he decided to hurt Abel and get rid of his competition. Or, when King Saul felt that the people liked David better than they like him after David killed the giant Philistine Goliath, he became so jealous that he came up with a plan to hunt David down and kill him. This week's Bible passage gives us another story of jealousy between Joseph and his brothers. Apparently, Joseph received all the attention and better treatment from his father. His brothers saw that and did not like it at all. They became jealous of Joseph and came up with a plan to get rid of him.

But, jealousy is not something that happened only in the Bible. It happens around us every day. When we see a friend has a new outfit or toy, we might want to have the same thing, and we become jealous of that person. That might cause us to take it from our friend, or at least feel as if we want to. Or, we might know someone who is popular in school, or has good looks, or is one that others treat more nicely than they treat us. So, we become jealous and might wish bad things would happen to that person. Jealousy causes people to do many crazy things; sometimes even hurt others badly.

Lord Jesus, I want to see

Jesus, Generous and Caring God, you were always generous in your thoughts and words toward everyone. You never wished harm or did bad things to anyone. Rather, you were always happy for someone if something great happened to that person. The best way for me to deal with jealousy is to be happy for everyone and their successes. I also need to be thankful and content with God's blessings in my life. With your example and support, I will try to live out what I just learned and hence bring about a world of love and peace.

My Promise

This week I will think of someone of whom I might be jealous or of something I might really want. Then, I will come to the Lord in prayer to give thanks for my life and try to find a reason to be happy for that person. Thank you, Jesus, Generous and Caring God. I love you!

Topic of the Week: Faith

"When Jesus had finished all His words to the people, He entered Capernaum. A centurion there had a slave who was ill and about to die, and he was valuable to him. When he heard about Jesus, he sent elders of the Jews to Him, asking Him to come and save the life of his slave. They approached Jesus and strongly urged Him to come, saying, 'He deserves to have you do this for him, for he loves our nation and he built the synagogue for us.' And Jesus went with them, but when He was only a short distance from the house, the centurion sent friends to tell Him, 'Lord, do not trouble yourself, for I am not worthy to have you enter under my roof. Therefore, I did not consider myself to come to you; but say the word and let my servant be healed. I am also a person subject to authority, with soldiers subject to me. And I say to one, 'Go,' and he goes; and to another, 'Come here,' and he comes; and to my slave, 'Do this, and he does it.' When Jesus heard this, He was amazed at him and, turning, He said to the crowd saying, 'I tell you, not even in Israel have I found such faith.' When the messengers returned to the house, they found the slave in good health." (Luke 7:1-10)

My Talk with Jesus

We often hear people say, "You have to have faith," "You better trust in God," or "Without faith, we cannot expect a miracle." Jesus always required a person to have faith in Him if that person really expected a miracle from Him. He also said, "Your faith has healed you," (Matthew 9:22) Faith is surely the way for us to get to Jesus and the Kingdom of God.

Faith usually brings us spectacular things also. Apparently, a centurion, in the story above, had a sick slave and heard a lot about the great miracle worker named Jesus. He decided to come to Him and believed that this great prophet could heal his slave. Unfortunately, he was not a Jew and did not know how to get Jesus to do him a favor. Thankfully, some elderly Jews recalled what the centurion did for the Jewish community, including building a synagogue for them, and decided to ask Jesus for help on his behalf. Jesus agreed to help the centurion and was quite impressed with his strong faith in Him. The centurion went home and was told that his slave was healed. A spectacular miracle happened because the centurion had faith in Jesus. Imagine how many wonderful things would come about for us if we simply put our faith in Him and pray.

Lord Jesus, I want to see

Jesus, My source of Hope and Salvation, you restored faith to many people and strengthened people with weak faith through your Good News and acts of love. Many people did not know where to put their trust after being driven into a life of slavery by their invaders, like the Romans, for many generations. They also felt hopeless in dealing with their personal problems every day. But you became the source of faith and hope for God's people. Sometimes, I feel like losing my faith living in this world, which is not friendly toward religion or supportive of one's devotion to God. My friends and school might make fun of my prayer life and discourage me from having a good relationship with God. Or, my prayers might not get answered right away or turn out the way I want. But with your help and encouragement, I will keep a good prayer life and a close friendship with you. I will also learn to put my faith in you and come to you often in prayer.

My Promise

This week I will come to you, Lord, and pray for someone who is really sick or desperately needs help. Then, I will leave everything in your hands with total faith and a humble spirit. Thank you, Jesus, My source of Hope and Salvation. I love you!

Topic of the Week: Holiness

"Jesus then went down to Capernaum, a town of Galilee. He taught them on the Sabbath, and they were astonished at His teaching because He spoke with authority. In the synagogue, there was a man with the spirit of an unclean demon, and he cried out in a loud voice, 'Ha! What have you to do with us, Jesus of Nazareth? Have you come to destroy us? I know who you are—the Holy One of God!' Jesus rebuked him and said, 'Be quiet! Come out of him!' Then the demon threw the man down in front of them and came out of him without doing him any harm. They were all amazed and said to one another, 'What is there about His word? For with authority and power He commands the unclean spirits, and they came out.' And news of Him spread everywhere in the surrounding region." (Luke 4:31-37)

My Talk with Jesus

Being holy is one of the greatest qualities of our God. Unfortunately, holiness is a quality that our world does not desire, nor does it see the great benefits of this quality in our day and age. This is why our world often does not care about God, faith, or religion. Worse yet, it might make fun of holiness or anyone who has a good relationship with God. But the Bible passage above tells us why holiness is such a wonderful quality for someone to have. Jesus went to a synagogue, and a man there with an evil spirit knew exactly who Jesus was and cried out in a loud voice, "... I know who you are—the Holy One of God! Have you come to destroy us?" That exclamation tells us a lot about Jesus and the importance of holiness in our world.

The unclean demon recognized Jesus' true identity and stated, "... You are the Holy One of God!" It also seemed to be afraid of the Holy One of God with this question, "... Have you come to destroy us?" What this means is that all demons and evil spirits are afraid of the Holy One of God or anything that is holy. So, holiness will help us recognize God and fight off all evil and dark power.

The Bible has many stories that show us the constant struggle between light and darkness, good and bad, holiness and evil. From the beginning of time, darkness has always hated light and wanted to get rid of it. Evil has constantly tried to defeat anything of holiness and put an end to it. Bad things also want to influence good things and tempt everyone to follow them. Fortunately, God is always in control and tries to protect the light, holiness, and good things from the attack of darkness, evil, and bad things. God sent His only son Jesus to defend children of the light and holiness from the power of darkness and evil. Sadly, much of the world has been tempted by the power of darkness and evil and followed it instead of God, who is the light and holiness.

Lord Jesus, I want to see

Jesus, source of Holiness and Goodness, you came into the world to show us the way to God and holiness. You also call us to avoid anything that is evil and bad. I might let the world tell me that it is all right to hang around evil and bad things. Or, I might believe those things will somehow bring me blessings and benefits in the long run. The truth is that nothing good can come from evil and bad things. These things will influence me negatively, cause me to do hurtful things, and eventually pull me away from God. That is why I need to stick close to God and search for things that are holy and good. For that is how I will find true happiness and many wonderful blessings from Heaven.

My Promise

This week I will try to avoid saying mean things and stay away from anything bad or evil. Instead, I will say more kind words to others and do only good and holy things. Thank you, Jesus, source of Holiness and Goodness. I love you!

SEPTEMBER

Lord Jesus,
I Want to See...

Topic of the Week: Friendship

"Jesus summoned his twelve disciples and gave them authority over unclean spirits to drive them out and to cure every disease and every illness. The names of the Apostles are these: First, Simon called Peter, and his brother Andrew; James, the son of Zebedee, and his brother John; Philip and Bartholomew; Thomas and Matthew the tax collector; James the son of Alphaeus, and Thaddeus; Simon the Cananean, and Judas Iscariot who betrayed Him. Jesus sent them out these twelve after instructing them thus, 'Do not go into pagan territory or enter a Samaritan town. Go rather to the lost sheep of the house of Israel. As you go, make this proclamation: 'The Kingdom of Heaven is at hand.' Cure the sick, raise the dead, cleanse the lepers, and drive out demons. Without cost you have received; without cost you are to give. Do not take gold or silver or copper for your belts, no sack for the journey, or a second tunic, or sandals, or walking stick. The laborer deserves his keep. Whatever town or village you enter, look for a worthy person in it, and stay there until you leave. As you enter a house, wish it peace..." (Matthew 10:1-15)

My Talk with Jesus

We all need friends besides our families. They bring us companionship, support, comfort, protection, guidance, love, help, and many other blessings. It would be extremely difficult for us to go through life without friendships. That is why Adam called out to God to give him a friend and was willing to sacrifice one of his ribs for it. God answered his request and created Eve for him.

The Bible passage above tells us how Jesus gathered His first twelve disciples who eventually became His friends. He needed these friends to help Him share His Good News with the world and do lots of good deeds. He sent them out two by two and gave them that important mission of salvation. So, besides bringing Jesus some companionship, His disciples also gave Him a hand with the mission work.

If Adam and Jesus needed some friendship, we surely must depend on our friends to survive here on earth. But, it is not easy to find the right friendships that will benefit us and last for a long time. As we might recall from the circle of friends surrounding Jesus, one of them, Judas, ended up betraying Him and sold Him to the authorities for thirty pieces of silver. That betrayal experience was so painful that Jesus wished He had never meet Judas at all. None of us wants to go through the same experience and get betrayed by a friend. Hopefully, this will compel us not to betray any of our friends and cause terrible hurt. Worse yet, we do not want to pick the wrong friends, who might lead us into trouble and become bad influences in our lives.

Lord Jesus, I want to see

Jesus, My Faithful and Thoughtful Friend, you tried to be a good friend to everyone and give a great example of loyal friendship for all of us. You once said, "Greater love has no one than this: to lay down one's life for one's friends." You practiced that by offering your own life on the Cross for us—your friends. I might not be able to do that for a friend yet. But, I hope I will be able to carry it out without any hesitation someday. For now, I will avoid any friendship that might lead me to do something bad. I will also try to be a faithful, good friend and make you my BFF.

My Promise

This week I will review my circle of friends with the help of prayer to see which friends will be a good influence on me and which ones will not. Then, I need to end my bad friendships and build up my good ones, while also trying to be a faithful friend. Thank you, Jesus, My Faithful and Thoughtful Friend. I love you!

Topic of the Week: Hardships

"… When the crowd saw that neither Jesus nor His disciples were there, they themselves got into boats and came to Capernaum looking for Jesus. And when they found Him across the Sea, they said to Him, 'Rabbi, when did you get here?' Jesus answered them and said, 'Amen, amen, I say to you, you are looking for me not because you saw signs, but because you ate the loaves and are filled. Do not work for food that perishes but for the food that endures for eternal life, which the Son of Man will give you… So, they said to Him, 'What can I do to accomplish the works of God?' Jesus said to them, 'Amen, amen, I say to you, it was not Moses who gave the bread from Heaven; my Father gives you the true bread from Heaven. For the bread of God is that which comes down from Heaven and gives life to the world.' So they said to Him, 'Sir, give us this bread always.' Jesus said to them, 'I am the bread of life; whoever comes to me will never hunger, and whoever believes in me will never thirst… I am the living bread that came down from Heaven, whoever eats this bread will live forever; and the bread that I will give is my flesh for the life of the world.' The Jews quarreled among themselves, saying, 'How can this man give us His flesh to eat?'… Then many of His disciples who were listening said, 'This saying is hard; who can accept it?' … As a result of this, many of His disciples returned to their former way of life and no longer accompanied Him. Jesus said to the Twelve, 'Do you also want to leave?' Simon Peter answered Him, 'Master, to whom shall we go? You have the words of eternal life. We have come to believe and are convinced that you are the Holy One of God.'" (John 6:22-69)

My Talk with Jesus

The Bible tells us that the journey to the Promised Land was difficult for God's people. They lost everything—from their country to their homes. They did not have enough to eat and drink along the journey. They also had to face dangers such as poisonous snakes. But, they always relied on the Lord and called on Him for help. Because of that relationship and their trust in the Lord, God's people could deal with those hardships and finally made it to the Promised Land to enjoy its blessings.

In this week's Bible passage, we are told that God's people found it difficult to believe that Jesus would give them His Body and Blood for nourishment. After Jesus' miracle of multiplication of the loaves and fish, God's people thought that they could keep on coming to Him and find a free lunch every day. But, Jesus tried to point them to spiritual nourishment. He told them that He would give them His Body and Blood as a source of that spiritual nourishment. Anyone who eats and drinks it will live forever. God's people could not believe in what Jesus said about His Body and Blood and began to laugh at Him.

Lord Jesus, I want to see

Jesus, My Guide and Nourishment, you had to face many hardships in your life from the moment of your birth, such as being born in an animals' manger. Yet, you never let your life's hardships make you bitter, unpleasant, or forsaken. I, too, have experienced some hardships in my life. But with your example and encouragement, I will not give up or run away from hardships. I will come to you often in prayers to ask for help and commit myself to overcome. For I believe my hardships will make me stronger and help me be more understanding and compassionate toward others around me.

My Promise

This week I will look for things I might find hard to do or understand, perhaps some subject at school. Then, I will come to you, Lord, in prayer and dedicate lots of time and efforts to that problem until things get a bit easier for me. Thank you, Jesus, My Guide and Nourishment. I love you!

Topic of the Week: Teaching

"When He saw the crowds, Jesus went up the mountain; and after He had sat down, His disciples came to Him. He began to teach them, saying: 'Blessed are the poor in spirit, for theirs is the Kingdom of Heaven. Blessed are they who mourn, for they will be comforted. Blessed are the meek, for they will inherit the land. Blessed are the merciful, for they will be shown mercy. Blessed are the clean of heart, for they will see God. Blessed are the peacemakers, for they will be called children of God. Blessed are they who are persecuted for the sake of righteousness, for theirs is the Kingdom of Heaven. Blessed are you when they insult you and persecute you and utter every kind of evil against you falsely because of me. Rejoice and be glad, for your reward will be great in Heaven.'" (Mt 5:1-12)

My Talk with Jesus

In life, we have certain people to whom we look for guidance and inspiration. We come to a teacher to help us learn and acquire good knowledge. We go see a counselor to share our problems and find answers. God's people also go to a Rabbi or a prophet to search for a good relationship with God and learn right from wrong. Jesus is a combination of all these types of people. People come to Him for all kinds of reasons: healing, feeding, learning, guidance, uplifting, encouraging, and so on. The Bible passage above was one of those occasions Jesus tried to teach and give God's people the right counsel about their daily living. He helped them find meaning in their suffering and strength to continue their journey of faith all the way to the Gate of Heaven.

We all have had certain teachers who have made a big difference in our lives. We remember fondly all the great advice and caring things these teachers did for us. Some of them have gone out of their way to spend extra time outside of the class to help us understand a problem. They have taught us right from wrong and how to make good decisions in life. They have shown us knowledge of the world and passed on to us experiences of people who have gone before us. They have comforted us when we had to deal with difficult problems. Teachers are like away-from-home parents who can help us grow in knowledge and wisdom and prepare us for the world.

Lord Jesus, I want to see

Jesus, Master and Teacher of the Truth, you taught and shared your Good News with God's people on many occasions, including the famous Sermon on the Mount that we see in this week's Bible passage. I think it might be fun to be a teacher, especially when one can speak loudly and boss others around! But, the truth is that there is lots of pressure and expectations on a teacher. I often do not realize this or appreciate the role of teachers in my life. They help shape, challenge, and encourage me to be the person that I will become tomorrow. I do not know where I would be if I didn't have teachers in my life. One thing is for sure, however—I would be ignorant and uneducated. I might not be the dedicated and hardworking person as I am now. Or, I might not have caring, understanding, and compassion as part of my personality if I had not been blessed with certain teachers in my life. I am thankful for all the teachers I have had in my years of education, most importantly Jesus, the best teacher of all.

My Promise

This week I will pray for all my teachers and recall some of the wonderful life lessons that they have taught me. I will also promise to show respect and listen to those who teach my classes that I attend this school year. Thank you, Jesus, Master and Teacher of the Truth. I love you!

Topic of the Week: Wisdom

"… In Gibeon, the Lord appeared to Solomon in a dream at night. God said, 'Ask something of me and I will give it to you.' Solomon answered: '… O Lord, my God, you have made me your servant, King to succeed my father David; but I am a mere youth, not knowing at all how to act. I serve you in the midst of the people whom you have chosen, a people so vast that it cannot be numbered or counted. Give your servant, therefore, an understanding heart to judge your people and to distinguish right from wrong. Who is able to govern this vast people of yours?' The Lord was pleased that Solomon made this request. So God said to him: 'Because you have asked for this—not for a long life for yourself, nor for riches, nor for the life of your enemies, but for understanding so that you may know what is right—I do as you requested. I give you a heart so wise and understanding that there has never been anyone like you up to now, and after you there will be no one to equal you… Later, two harlots came to the King and stood before him… Then, the King said: 'One woman claims, 'This, the living one, is my child, and the dead one is yours.' The other answers, 'No! The dead one is you child; the living one is mine.' The King continued, 'Get me a sword.' When they brought the sword before him, he said, 'Cut the living child two, and give half to one woman and half to the other.' The woman whose son it was, in the anguish she felt for it, said to the King, 'Please my Lord, give her the living child—please do not kill it!' The other, however said, 'It shall be neither mine nor yours. Divide it!' The King then answered, 'Give the first one the living child! By no means kill it, for she is the mother.'... The people saw that the King had in him the wisdom of God for giving judgment." (1 Kings 3)

My Talk with Jesus

The Bible passage above tells us that King Solomon asked God for Wisdom, used that precious gift from God to govern his Kingdom, and found the truth in a dispute over a baby. Apparently, two women gave birth to two babies. Unfortunately, one baby died, and its mother tried to claim her ownership over the living child. If they had the DNA technology that we have now, they could determine to whom the babies belonged. Because they did not have either of those tools, they had to rely on the Wisdom of King Solomon to resolve this emotional case. When King Solomon suggested dividing the baby, the baby's real mother spoke up, because she did not want her child hurt. In this way, King Solomon could identify the baby's real mother. He knew the real mother would not allow her baby to be hurt.

Lord Jesus, I want to see

Jesus, source of Wisdom and Truth, you showed God's people many wise teachings and miracles. Whoever heard your teachings felt comforted, uplifted, strengthened, and encouraged. Your words of wisdom also brought hope to and helped save lots of lives. Our current culture thinks a person must be smart with computer and technology. Schools and learning centers these days only teach book knowledge and pass on information to our young. But, they forgot to teach them about life experiences and pass on Wisdom of the past generations. I do not know about the rest of the world, but I want to search for the Wisdom of God and learn about God's ways. I want to be a wise person who knows right from wrong and good from bad. I want to secure an eternal life in Heaven!

My Promise

This week I will search for the Wisdom of God in prayer, in reading the Bible, and by listening to a well-respected person. I will also try to make wise choices by only doing good things and avoiding wrong things. Thank you, Jesus, source of Wisdom and Truth. I love you!

OCTOBER

Lord Jesus, I Want to See...

Topic of the Week: Cheating

"When Isaac was so old that his eyesight had failed him, he called his older son Esau and said to him, 'Son!' 'Yes, father!' he replied. Isaac then said, 'As you can see, I am so old that I may now die at any time. Take your gear, therefore—your quiver and bow—and go out into the country to hunt some game for me. With your catch prepare an appetizing dish for me, such as I like, and bring it to me to eat, so that I may give you my special blessing before I die.' Rebekah had been listening while Isaac was speaking to his son Esau. So when Esau went out into the country to hunt some game for his father, Rebekah said to her son Jacob, 'Listen! I overheard your father tell your brother Esau, 'Bring me some game and with it prepare an appetizing dish for me to eat, that I may give you blessing with the Lord's approval before I die.' Now son, listen carefully to what I tell you. Go to the flock and get me two choice kids. With these I will prepare an appetizing dish for your father, such as he likes. Then bring it to your father to eat, that he may bless you before he dies.' 'But my brother Esau is a hairy man,' said Jacob to his mother Rebekah, 'and I am smooth-skinned! Suppose my father feels me?' ... So Jacob went and got the choice kids from the flock and brought them to his mother so she prepared an appetizing dish, such as his father liked. Rebekah then took the best clothes of her older son Esau that she had in the house, and gave them to her younger son Jacob to wear; ... Isaac then said to Jacob, 'Come closer, son, that I may feel you, to learn whether you really are my son Esau or not.' So, Jacob moved up closer to his father. When Isaac felt him, he said, 'Although the voice is Jacob's, the hands are Esau's ... Then Isaac said, 'Serve me your game, son, that I may eat of it and then give you my blessing.' Jacob served it to him, and Isaac ate; he brought him wine, and he drank … With that, he blessed Jacob…" (Genesis 27)

My Talk with Jesus

The Bible passage above shares with us how Jacob was chosen to receive the blessing of his father Isaac. In Jewish tradition, when the father of a family grows old and gets close to his time of death, he likes to give a special blessing and pass on the family tradition to the next generation. Usually, that special honor goes to the oldest male of the household. But, Isaac's wife, Rebekah, seemed to favor her youngest son Jacob over the oldest son, Esau. She decided to get Jacob dressed up like his brother Esau so that he could get the special blessing from his father, Isaac. She also helped Jacob prepare the favorite dish for his father, all while Esau was out hunting. Although Isaac had the feeling that he was tricked, he still gave Jacob his blessing. Although we were taught that cheating is wrong, God used this unfortunate swap of the two brothers and chose Jacob to be the next leader of God's people.

Lord Jesus, I want to see

Jesus, My Guide and Support, you taught your disciples to do the right things and avoid the wrong ones. That is how they stayed close to you as the source of goodness and kept away from anything evil. I sometimes think it is all right to cheat, or it is no big deal to do something bad. But, the reality is that I am not God, and I cannot turn something bad into something good. What I need to focus on always is to do good and kind things and avoid bad and evil things. When I follow that simple rule, I will always receive God's blessings. I will not have to worry whether God will need to intervene and help me turn something bad into good. So, I choose to stay away from cheating.

My Promise

This week I will see if I have cheated on someone or something lately. Then, I will stop that bad act and do something good to make up for it. Thank you, Jesus, My Guide and Support. I love you!

Topic of the Week: Failure

"Getting into one of the boats, the one belonging to Simon, he [Jesus] asked him to put out a short distance from the shore. Then he sat down and taught the crowds from the boat. After he had finished speaking, he said to Simon, 'Put out into deep water and lower your nets for a catch.' Simon said in reply, 'Master, we have worked hard all night and have caught nothing, but at your command I will lower the nets.' When they had done this, they caught a great number of fish and their nets were tearing. They signaled to their partners in the other boat to come to help them. They came and filled both boats so that they were in danger of sinking. When Simon Peter saw this, he fell at the knees of Jesus and said, 'Depart from me, Lord, for I am a sinful man.' For astonishment at the catch of fish they had made seized him and those with him..." (Luke 5:1-11)

My Talk with Jesus

None of us wants to fail. It is often difficult for us to see ourselves fail and admit it. For failure means humiliation and loss. The Bible passage above tells us a story of Peter, who was a professional fisherman, but had to face a tough fishing night at sea and caught nothing. He was tired, frustrated, and hopeless. He must have felt like a failure after spending a long night at sea and coming home empty. He did not know what to do next to change his misfortune or what tomorrow might bring. Thankfully, Jesus showed up to give him a hand and asked him to put out the nets in deep water on the right side of the boat. After such a long and exhausting night of failure, Peter could have refused to listen to Jesus. Besides, he was a professional fisherman and Jesus was not. But, Peter decided to follow Jesus' suggestion, and the result was a successful catch. He filled up two boats with fish to the point of almost sinking! As we can see, if we listen to God's guidance and allow God to help us, we can turn our failure into success and enjoy a new life.

We will surely run into failures at some point in our lives. We could fail a test and get a bad grade or fail to understand a class subject and become frustrated in that class. Or, maybe we fail to win a game against another team and get upset with that loss. Or we may fail to do certain tasks given to us and cause disappointment to people in authority. Maybe we fail to make friends with some people and begin to harbor hurt feelings. These failures might cause ugly emotions to surface, including sadness and depression. But, our Christian faith and the Bible story above remind us to find help and hope for our failures in the Lord Jesus.

Lord Jesus, I want to see

Jesus, My Hope and Salvation, you helped thousands of people who have felt they were a failure and their lives had hit a dead end. You brought hope and restored confidence to all their lives. These people are forever grateful for your miraculous work. I sometimes think I can do anything and then find myself to be a failure when things do not turn out my way. Besides, our current culture tries to convince me that there is nothing you can do to help me. However, I know from my Christian faith and the Bible story above that you are always ready to help me if I am open to it. I will look up to you for a solution when I seem to fail at something, and I will never give up.

My Promise

This week I will see where I might have fail recently and then bring that problem to you, Lord, in prayer to find a solution and guidance. That way, you can talk to me and show me what I need to do next. Thank you, Jesus, My Hope and Salvation. I love you!

Topic of the Week: Listening

"As they continued their journey, He [Jesus] entered a village where a woman whose name was Martha welcomed Him. She had a sister named Mary who sat beside the Lord at His feet listening to Him speak. Martha, burdened with much serving, came to Him and said, 'Lord, do you not care that my sister has left me by myself to do the serving? Tell her to help me.' The Lord said to her in reply, 'Martha, Martha, you are anxious and worried about many things. There is need of only one thing. Mary has chosen the better part, and it will not be taken from her.'" (Luke 10:38-42)

My Talk with Jesus

It is not easy for anyone to sit and listen to someone for any length of time. Most of us cannot sit still and focus on something. But, there is someone who we all would love to be around and spend time with. That someone is Jesus Himself. If we could listen and hang around Jesus a little more, we might learn how to achieve a happy life on earth and prepare for ourselves an eternal life in Heaven.

Listening to our teachers and paying attention in a class is difficult. We all want to chat with our friends and people around us. Listening to our parents and doing what they ask is difficult also, because we like to play and do our own things. Certainly, listening is not a skill with which we were born. It is something we need to learn and practice. It might take years for us to gain this skill and become a great listener. But, once this skill is ours, it will benefit us a great deal and make us a better person. Once we learn to listen, we can listen to God and others around us with care. When our families or friends have problems in their lives, they can come and share with us their sorrows and know that we listen and care about them.

When we are a good listener, we can listen to God in addition to people. We can focus on hearing what God wants us to do every day, such as doing good things and avoiding evil things; working up to our potential and trying to help others more; or being a person of love and peace instead of hatred and violence. Mary was a good listener and knew the importance of listening to God. She chose to spend time at the feet of Jesus instead of running around like her sister Martha. She wanted to listen to every word that came from the mouth of Jesus. She knew that He had words of comfort, peace, love, hope, joy, and life.

Lord Jesus, I want to see

Jesus, the Word and the Voice of God, thousands of people came to listen to you every day. The famous crowd that gathered around you for your wisdom was the one that you talked about in the Beatitudes (Matthew 5:1-12). In that speech, you blessed and lifted up the lowly and the poor with the promise of the Kingdom of Heaven. I might find it difficult to listen to you during prayer time and in Church. I might think my time with you in prayer is boring and useless. What I need to realize is that Mary in the Bible passage above and thousands of people in the Gospels came to listen to you because they got something out of it. They were looking for your words of hope and wisdom. Help me learn to value your words and listen to you in my daily prayers, in the people I meet, or in the events that happen around me.

My Promise

This week I will try to spend time in prayer every day and listen to your messages for me in those moments and other events happening around me. So, speak Lord, for I am listening. Thank you, Jesus, the Word and the Voice of God. I love you!

Topic of the Week: Help

"... When it was reported to the King of Egypt that the people had fled, Pharaoh and his servants changed their minds about them. 'What have we done?' they exclaimed. 'Why, we have released Israel from our service!' ...So the Egyptians then pursued them; Pharaoh's whole army, his horses, chariots, and charioteers caught up with them as they lay encamped by the sea... Pharaoh was already near when the Israelites looked up and saw that the Egyptians were on the march in pursuit of them. In great fright, they cried out to the Lord. And they complained to Moses, 'Were there no burial places in Egypt that you had to bring us out here to die in the desert? ...' But, Moses answered the people, 'Fear not! Stand your ground, and you will see the victory the Lord will win for you today. These Egyptians whom you see today you will never see again. The Lord Himself will fight for you; you have only to keep still.' ... Then Moses stretched out his hand over the sea, and the Lord swept the sea with a strong east wind throughout the night and so turned it into dry land. When the water was thus divided, the Israelites marched into the midst of the sea on dry land, with the water like a wall to their right and to their left. The Egyptians followed in pursuit; all Pharaoh's horses and chariots and charioteers went after them right into the midst of the sea... Moses stretched out his hand over the Sea, and at dawn the sea flowed back to its normal depth... As the water flowed back, it covered the chariots and the charioteers of Pharaoh's whole army, which had followed the Israelites into the sea. Not a single one of them escaped. But, the Israelites had marched on dry land through the midst of the sea... Thus, the Lord saved Israel on that day from the power of the Egyptians..." (Exodus 14)

My Talk with Jesus

We humans need all the help we can get, especially from above. We believers can come to God to ask for help and protection. That is exactly what God's people did in the Bible story above as they relied on Moses to call on God to help free them from the Egyptians and slavery. Unfortunately, Pharaoh and the Egyptians decided to chase after God's people and bring them back as slaves. Without a moment of delay, God performed one of the greatest miracles of all time and led His people through the Red Sea. After God's people made it through the sea, God closed up the sea and destroyed the whole Egyptian army that was pursuing them. God was the only help for God's people in their desperate time, and soon they realized that they could come to God anytime and anywhere to ask for help.

That must be the attitude that we Christians should have at all times and come to God for help at any time. Unfortunately, some of us have decided to follow the world and ask it for help instead of God. But, the world only pretends to help us and does not follow through with its promises. On the other hand, our God is faithful to us and makes sure we get all the help we need.

Lord Jesus, I want to see

Jesus, My Helper and Protector, you came to the rescue of many people and gave them a helping hand during your ministry. God's people recognized the wonderful source of help you brought them and came to look for you constantly in a big crowd. I might not want to bother you or might forget to turn to you for help and guidance. But, I need to start coming to you and asking for help in doing my daily duties. I will also ask you to help my family, friends, and neighbors in times of need and troubles, for you love to help anyone in need.

My Promise

This week I will come to you, Lord, in prayer and ask for help about some trouble I might have in school, at home, or with a friend. Thank you, Jesus, My Helper and Protector. I love you!

NOVEMBER

Lord Jesus, I Want to See...

Topic of the Week: Promise

"... The words of the Lord came to him [Abraham]: 'No, that one shall not be your heir; your own issue shall be your heir.' He [the Lord] took him outside and said, 'Look up at the sky and count the stars, if you can. Just so,' He added, 'shall your descendants be.' Abram put his faith in the Lord, who credited it to him as an act of righteousness... Then the Lord said to Abram: 'Know for certain that your descendants shall be aliens in a land not their own, where they shall be enslaved and oppressed for four hundred years. But, I will bring judgment on the nation they must serve and in the end, they will depart with great wealth. You, however, shall join your forefathers in peace; you shall be buried at a contented old age. In the fourth time-span, the others shall come back here; the wickedness of the Amorites will not have reached its full measure until then.' When the sun had set and it was dark, there appeared a smoking brazier and a flaming torch, which passed between those pieces. It was on that occasion that the Lord made a covenant with Abram, saying: 'To your descendants I give this land...'" (Genesis 15)

My Talk with Jesus

Abraham was a faithful servant of the Lord. He always followed what the Lord commanded and was also kind and generous to God's people. Because of his virtuous way of life, the Lord made a great Promise to him that his descendants would be as abundant as the stars in the sky. The Lord also promised him and his descendants a wonderful piece of land that would be easy for them to plant and harvest. Although the

Lord made that great Promise, Abraham and God's people still ran into lots of hardships along the way. For example, Abraham and his wife Sarah could not bear any children. Meanwhile, God's people were constantly attacked by their enemies and driven into slavery. With that much hardship, it would take years before God's Promise for Abraham and God's people came true.

People make promises all the time, but often do not follow through with them. Sadly, we Christians slowly become like the rest of the world and make empty promises without any regret at all. We tell our families that we will do certain tasks that they ask of us, but we end up not doing them at all. Or, we promise our friends that we will do something for them like keeping a secret, but we break that promise and tell someone else. Or, we promise to talk with God in prayer and do good for others daily, but we get distracted by other things and forget to go through with it. When we break our promises or fail to do them, over time that becomes a bad habit, and we simply lie to others about what we might do.

Lord Jesus, I want to see

Jesus, My source of Help and Truth, you made God's promise of salvation come true for our world by coming to earth. Your whole ministry on earth, however, was not about making one promise after another. Rather, you made God's promise of eternal life a reality and brought a taste of Heaven to thousands of people. I might imitate the ways of the world and make lots of empty promises. But, you want me to follow your example and make lots of my promises to my family and friends come true. I can help my family become more loving and joyful by not fighting with my siblings and helping more around the house. I can make God's presence in the world more real by encouraging my family and friends to reach out and help more people in need.

My Promise

This week, I will examine closely what I promised my family and friends. Then, I will make sure those promises come true by rolling up my sleeves and trying to do all the necessary work. Thank you, Jesus, My source of Help and Truth. I love you!

Topic of the Week: Care

"... On the third day there was a wedding in Cana in Galilee, and the mother of Jesus was there. Jesus and His disciples were also invited to the wedding. When the wine ran short, the mother of Jesus said to Him, 'They have no wine.' Jesus said to her, 'Woman, how does your concern affect me? My hour has not yet come.' His mother said to the servers, 'Do whatever He tells you.' Now there were six water jars there for Jewish ceremonial washings, each holding twenty to thirty gallons. Jesus told them, 'Fill the jars with water.' So they filled them to the brim. Then He told them, 'Draw some out now and take it to the headwaiter.' So they took it. And when the headwaiter tasted the water that had become wine, without knowing where it came from (although the servers who had drawn the water knew), the headwaiter called the bridegroom and said to him, 'Everyone serves good wine first, and then when people have drunk freely, an inferior one; but you have kept the good wine until now.' Jesus did this as the beginning of His signs in Cana in Galilee and so revealed His glory, and His disciples began to believe in Him.'" (John 2:1-11)

My Talk with Jesus

When someone shows us that he/she cares about us and our well-being, it makes us feel good. At school, a teacher who cares about our learning will get us to feel the same and motivate us to work hard, even if some lessons are difficult to understand. A caring teacher will go out of his/her way to show us something that we might not quite understand. Similarly, a caring coach, nurse, doctor, or friend will make a big difference in our lives and encourage us to do the right things. In fact, our world would be a better place if there are more caring people. The problem with our world these days is that most people do not care about anything or anyone any more. All they care about is themselves and their selfish desires. That is why we see constant outbursts and senseless violence all around us.

Unlike those angry and violent folks, Jesus in the Gospel passage above showed us how generous and caring He was to everyone, even to strangers like people at the wedding in Cana. Although He did not know the wedding couple and their guests, Jesus had such a caring and generous heart that He went out of His way to help them. He performed His first miracle and turned water into wine even though He was not quite ready to roll out His ministry plan. He let the whole world see the power of a caring and generous heart. Our world would be a better place if there are more people like Jesus.

Lord Jesus, I want to see

Jesus, My Caring Friend and Loving God, you never hesitated to reach out and care for others, especially the misfortunate and the outcast. Your big heart touched so many people in your short time of ministry and changed our world for the better. I am sometimes tempted by the world to have a cold heart and uncaring attitude. Some people around me might try to convince me that I do not need to care for anyone else except myself. However, you challenge me to change the world around me not by doing something popular, but by having a caring heart. I need to help the world change from the inside by having a caring heart and a generous spirit. I am sure if everyone had such a heart and spirit, our world would be much different than what I see now.

My Promise

This week I will see if someone around me at home or school needs my helping hand and caring heart. Then, I will make personal sacrifices and reach out to help that person without expecting anything in return. Thank you, Jesus, My Caring Friend and Loving God. I love you!

Topic of the Week: Thankfulness

"As Jesus continued His journey to Jerusalem, He traveled through Samaria and Galilee. As He was entering a village, ten lepers met Him. They stood at a distance from Him and raised their voice, saying, 'Jesus Master! Have pity on us!' And when He saw them, He said, 'Go show yourselves to the priests.' As they were going, they were cleansed. And one of them, realizing he had been healed, returned, glorifying God in a loud voice; and he fell at the feet of Jesus and thanked Him. He was a Samaritan. Jesus said in reply, 'Ten were cleansed, were they not? Where are the other nine? Has none but this foreigner returned to give thanks to God?' Then He said to him, 'Stand up and go; your faith has saved you.'" (Luke 17:11-19)

My Talk with Jesus

Thanksgiving is usually a fun, family event when everyone gathers and shares a big turkey banquet and other bonding activities such as watching a football game or going shopping on Black Friday. Not too long ago, Thanksgiving was supposed to be a time for the early settlers in this country to come together with Native Americans to give thanks to God for a successful fall harvest and share a simple meal together. Over the years, the whole idea of giving thanks to God as the focus for the Thanksgiving celebration has been slowly diminished and replaced with other popular activities of our time. It is very rare these days to have a family that gathers at Thanksgiving to say "Thank you" to God and one another. Many people today are not grateful for what they have and do not hesitate to take things from others by force and violence.

Realizing how important it is to have a thanksgiving attitude, Jesus pointed out to us in the Bible passage above how disappointed He was to see only one out of the ten lepers that He healed came back to give thanks to God. That means that ninety percent of the lepers were never grateful to God for what God had done for them. That is sad, isn't it? Worst yet, the only thankful leper was not a devout Jew. If an unbeliever like this leper knew how to return to give thanks, shouldn't we do the same and come to God every day to show gratitude for our daily blessings?

A grateful person is thoughtful, considerate, decent, caring, understanding, loving, and merciful. Those qualities make a normal person a saint, and everyone wants to hang around a saintly person. Such a person makes us feel better and influences us positively. Our society would be a Heavenly place if its members were grateful people. There would be less complaining, criticizing, fighting, disrupting, and violent behavior in our world. Instead, there could be more appreciating, encouraging, caring, uplifting, and peacefulness.

Lord Jesus, I want to see

Jesus, My Helper and Protector, you were happy to drive away evil spirits and give a helping hand to God's people. But, you would be happy if everyone that you assisted came to God and said "Thank you" for what God had done for them. I have been blessed with so many good things in my life. I continue to receive many of your blessings each day. Yet, I have been a bit slow to show my gratitude to you. I need to say "Thank you" to you every day and learn to share your blessings with others who might be less fortunate. That is how I can make you proud.

My Promise

This week, I will try to say “Thank you” to you Lord at least once a day for God’s blessings in my life. Then, I will try to pay it forward by doing some good deeds for others. Thank you, Jesus, My Helper and Protector. I love you!

Topic of the Week: Home

"In the first year of Cyrus, King of Persia, in order to fulfill the word of the Lord spoken by Jeremiah, the Lord inspired King Cyrus of Persia to issue this proclamation throughout his Kingdom, both by word of mouth and in writing: 'Thus says Cyrus, King of Persia: 'All the Kingdoms of the earth the Lord, the God of Heaven, has given to me, and He has also charged me to build him a house in Jerusalem, which is in Judah. Whoever, therefore, among you belongs to any part of His people, let him go up; and may his God be with him! Let everyone who has survived, in whatever place he may have dwelt, be assisted by the people of that place with silver, gold, goods, and cattle, together with free-will offerings for the house of God in Jerusalem." Then the family heads of Judah and Benjamin and the priests and Levites— everyone, that is, whom God has inspired to do so—prepared to go up to build the house of the Lord in Jerusalem. All their neighbors gave them help in every way, with silver, gold, goods, and cattle, and with many precious gifts besides all their free-will offerings. King Cyrus too had the utensils of the house of the Lord brought forth, which Nebuchadnezzar had taken away from Jerusalem and placed in the house of his god..." (Ezra 1:1-11)

My Talk with Jesus

Some wise person once said, "There is no place like home." Home is where we feel most at ease and can be who we are. In most cases, we can do whatever we would like to do at home. We do not have to pretend to be someone else to make ourselves look good. That is why people always want to be home after being all over the world, even when they visit famous and beautiful places.

That is exactly how God's people felt after being driven into slavery for years. They lost everything, including their possessions, homes, and country. They certainly did not know when they would be able to come home. Some perhaps thought they would never see their homes again. But, the Bible passage above tells us how God's people received the greatest news of their lives. King Cyrus of Persia, their captor, decided to set them free and let them return home. Along with their freedom, the King also gave back their possessions and helped them rebuild the Temple of the Lord in Jerusalem. Now God's people could come home and rebuild their lives.

Most of us have not been through an awful experience like God's people endured back then. We might take our home for granted and not realize how it must feel to lose the security of our house. But, our homes on earth are not permanent and are often referred to as a tent by St. Paul. What St. Paul meant to say is that our homes on earth do not last forever. Our true home is in Heaven. In that place, we can truly feel safe, and no one can take it away from us. That is why we Christians look forward to making our home in Heaven where we can meet Jesus and be with Him forever.

Lord Jesus, I want to see

Jesus, My Shelter and Fortress, you always tried to protect and watch over God's people during your ministry on earth. You are the true home for me to seek shelter on earth and in Heaven. I might not fully realize that about you or maybe I take my home for granted. But, today, it is time for me to find my true home in you. It is time for me to take good care of my home by not fighting with my siblings, by helping more around the house, and by bringing more love and peace to my family.

My Promise

This week I will think of something that will show I am grateful for having a home. Then, I will do something to take good care of my home. Thank you, Jesus, My Shelter and Fortress. I love you!

DECEMBER

Lord Jesus, I Want to See...

Topic of the Week: Angel

"Now there were shepherds in that region living in the fields and keeping the night watch over their flock. The angel of the Lord appeared to them and the glory of the Lord shone around them, and they were struck with great fear. The angel said to them, 'Do not be afraid; for behold, I proclaim to you good news of great joy that will be for all the people. For today in the city of David, a Savior has been born for you who is Messiah and Lord. And this will be a sign for you: You will find an infant wrapped in swaddling clothes and lying in a manger.' And suddenly there was a multitude of the heavenly host with the angel, praising God and saying: 'Glory to God in the highest and on earth peace to those on whom his favor rests.' When the angels went away from them to Heaven, the shepherds said to one another, 'Let us go, then, to Bethlehem to see this thing that has taken place, which the Lord has made known to us. So, they went in haste and found Mary and Joseph, and the infant lying in the manger. When they saw this, they made known the message that has been told to them about this child. All who heard it were amazed by what had been told them by the shepherds. And Mary kept all these things, reflecting on them in her heart..." (Luke 2:8-20)

My Talk with Jesus

We have heard about and see pictures of angel everywhere. People believe that angels are all around us and continue to seek help from them. The Bible passage above is one of the familiar stories about angels that is told around Christmas time. It tells us how the angels appeared to the shepherds in the fields at midnight and announced to them the birth of Jesus, the Son of God. They also sang the "Gloria" along with the choirs of angels—Cherubim and Seraphim—and led the shepherd to the manger where Baby Jesus was found. Like the Archangel Gabriel, who came to Mary to let her know about her conception of Jesus, these angels were sent to let the whole world know about the joyous birth of Baby Jesus.

But, angels do more than simply bring messages of joyous news. They are also sent to give people warning messages and protect them. St. Joseph, the foster father of Jesus, was told by an angel in a dream to take Baby Jesus and Mary to Egypt to avoid the persecution of King Herod. We Christians also believe that each of us has been given a Guardian Angel to protect, guide, and help us make the right decisions in life. The final image of an angel in our Christian faith is the Archangel Michael, who is assigned to blow the trumpet on the Last Day and call up all the dead for God's Judgment.

Lord Jesus, I want to see

Jesus, Son of God and Savior of the World, several times during your ministry, you mentioned your belief in angels and their presence in this world and the next. I might or might not have seen an angel with my own eyes. But, sometimes people talk about a person who came to their rescue in a time of need or danger, like an angel. I am sure I have met many kind and courageous people like that in my life. They might not look like an angel with wings and the ability to fly. Yet, their angel-like actions toward someone like me in a time of need or danger tells me that they are angels sent to give me a hand. I thank you for giving me these angels in my life. I want to imitate their example and try to be an angel to other people around me who might be facing a difficult time.

My Promise

This week, I will look for someone around me who might need help. Then, I will reach out to give that person a helping hand—like an angel—and bring him/her some comfort by listening to his/her anguish and worries. Thank you, Jesus, Son of God and Savior of the world. I love you!

Topic of the Week: Darkness

"For God so loved the world that He gave His only Son, so that everyone who believes in Him might not perish but might have eternal life. For God did not send His Son into the world to condemn it; but the world might be saved through Him. Whoever believes in Him will not be condemned; but whoever does not believe has already been condemned, because he has not believed in the name of the only Son of God. And this is the verdict, that the Light came into the world, but people preferred Darkness to Light, because their works were evil. For everyone who does wicked things hates the Light and does not come toward the Light, so that his works might not be exposed. But whoever lives the truth comes to the light, so that his works may be clearly seen as done in God." (John 3:16-21)

My Talk with Jesus

Darkness is surely all around us. Half of our 24-hour day, in fact, is spent in darkness. If we look out into the universe or deep into the ocean, we will realize that they are pitch dark. Without light or the sun, our world would be totally swallowed up by darkness. Certainly, we all feel scared and lost in the dark. While we humans are fearful of darkness, there are certain things that thrive in darkness. Creepy, crawly creatures like spiders, scorpions, worms, maggots, roaches, snakes, bats, and so on often hide in the dark and enjoy any place of darkness. The creatures that like darkness the most are the Devil and evil spirits. These creatures were condemned by God to the underworld or Hell, where there is darkness and suffering.

Realizing how desperate our world needed some light, God sent God's Son to bring it light. For that, we might think our world would have rolled out the red carpet to welcome God's Son. Instead, our world rejected Him and did everything it could to keep His light from entering. In fact, the world crucified Him on the Cross and buried Him in a tomb. The Bible passage above shows us the continuous struggle between light and darkness and how our world has kept the light of Christ from shining in it. This is exactly what we see happening in our world right now. Some angry folks have decided to take out their frustrations on others, and some randomly shoot innocent people around them. Terrorists and evil folks do not like all the good works of loving and peaceful people and hence they do anything they can to destroy them. Meanwhile, people continue to cheat, steal, be selfish, be greedy, and act mean to one another. They also do not want to follow God's Law and do the right things.

Lord Jesus, I want to see

Jesus, the source of Light and Goodness, you not only brought light into our world but also showed us all the good things we can do for God and one another. That is how you bring our world of darkness closer to the light and make it a better place. I surely do not want our world to remain in darkness and for people to continue to hurt one another. I definitely do not want to participate in the world of darkness and promote it. If anything, I need to help reduce darkness in our world by adding more light to it with many kind words and good deeds. If more people tried to do that, our dark world would turn bright in no time.

My Promise

This week, I will see how I have contributed to the world of darkness with any mean attitudes, bad words, or evil acts. Then, I will try to add more light to the world by saying only kind words, being thoughtful to others, and doing good deeds. Thank you, Jesus, the source of Light and Goodness. I love you!

Topic of the Week: Light

"You are the Light of the world. A city set on a mountain cannot be hidden. Nor do they light a lamp and then put it under a bushel basket; it is set on a lampstand, where it gives Light to all the house. Just so, your Light must shine before others, that they may see your deeds and glorify your Heavenly Father." (Matthew 5:14-16)

My Talk with Jesus

Thankfully, half of our day is in the light. Without light or the sun, our world would be completely engulfed by darkness. Nothing would be able to grow. Everything would turn dark, cold, and dead. Light helps bring heat, joy, motivation, safety, and guidance into our lives. It shows us the way and makes us feel safe and secure. We can see where we are going and will not run into things or one another. The Prince of Darkness and evil spirits can no longer trick us or scare us when our world is filled with the light. When we are around the light, we feel safe, confident, joyful, and uplifted. Light basically makes us feel as if we are in the presence of God. Nothing in this world or the world of darkness can make us fearful when we are surrounded by the light.

Our world is filled with the brightest light around Christmas. Everything is bright and clear around this time of the year. Every household and dark corner of the earth is filled with colorful lights and Christmas decorations to welcome the Light and Special Guest of the Season, Jesus. But, we Christians also believe that Jesus is the Light and Savior of the world. He came to earth to bring us eternal light and show us the way to

Heaven. In the Bible passage above, we are called to put the Light on a lampstand—just like other lights in our household—so that it can shine brightly throughout the house and benefit everyone. Unfortunately, many Christians have hidden the Light of Christ under a bushel basket and have kept it away from our dark world—a world that is in desperate need of it. When we do that, we allow the Prince of Darkness and evil spirits to continue keeping our world in darkness.

There is another way we have kept the Light of Christ under bushel basket: we stop doing good deeds in the name of Christ or do not care for and love our neighbors as Christ would. If our world cannot see the Light of Christ through our good deeds, it will continue to live in darkness and fear. We need to spread the Light of Christ throughout the world by doing good deeds and lots of caring and loving acts. Imagine how bright and safe our world would be if everyone reflected the Light of Christ.

Lord Jesus, I want to see

Jesus, My Light and Salvation, you did not come to condemn our dark world and push it away. Rather, you came to bring it light and show it the way to God and Heaven. Everyone who met you during your ministry saw and found a completely new vision because of your light. I sometimes feel scared and lost in this world because of the darkness that surrounds me. Or, I sometimes feel embarrassed about letting the light of Christ shine brightly through me. With your encouragement, I will try hard each day to let your light shine throughout the world with my kind words and loving acts. I will also avoid any mean words, a bad attitude, and evil acts that might make our world become dark and scary.

My Promise

This week I will avoid anything that might make our world dark and miserable such as lying to my parents and teachers, fighting with my siblings, or telling bad rumors about my friends. Instead, I will say only kind things and do at least one good deed a day this week to bring the Light of Christ to the world. Thank you, Jesus, my Light and Salvation. I love you!

Topic of the Week: Jesus

"In the sixth month, the angel Gabriel was sent from God to a town of Galilee called Nazareth, to a virgin betrothed to a man named Joseph, of the house of David, and the virgin's name was Mary. And coming to her he said, 'Hailed, favored one! The Lord is with you.' But she was greatly troubled at what was said and pondered what sort of greeting this might be. Then the angel said to her, 'Do not be afraid, Mary, for you have found favor with God. Behold, you will conceive in your womb and bear a son, and you shall name Him Jesus. He will be great and will be called Son of the Most High, and the Lord God will give Him the throne of David His Father, and He will rule over the house of Jacob forever, and of His Kingdom there will be no end.' ... All went to be enrolled, each to his own town. And Joseph too went up from Galilee from the town of Nazareth to Judea, to the city of David that is called Bethlehem, because he was of the house and family of David, to be enrolled with Mary, his betrothed, who was with child. While they were there, the time came for her to have her child, and she gave birth to her first-born son. She wrapped him in swaddling clothes and laid him in a manger, because there was no room for them in the inn..." (Luke 1:26-2:20)

My Talk with Jesus

In case we have forgotten how Jesus came into our world, this week's Bible passage tells us about His humble birth. First, the Archangel Gabriel told Mary that she would become the mother of Jesus, who would be conceived by the Holy Spirit. Then, she was married to Joseph. Next, this young couple went to Bethlehem where Mary gave birth to Baby Jesus in a manger because they could find no room in the inn. Baby Jesus then grew in wisdom and God's power was with Him. He went from towns to villages to preach the Good News of the Kingdom of God, heal the sick, feed the hungry, and give new life to the dead and hopeless. He performed many miracles and was the Messiah for which God's people had been waiting.

But, Jesus was not the political leader for which they were hoping. Instead, He became a servant leader who washed their feet, served their needs, and ultimately offered His own life on the Cross to save them from being punished for their sins. He was taken down from the Cross and buried in a tomb, but rose on the third day. He did a lot of great work for God's people during His three years of ministry on earth, including His teachings of the Beatitudes and Commandments of love: love God and love our neighbors. He showed the world the way to true happiness and eternal life.

Lord Jesus, I want to see

Jesus, My Best Friend and Savior, you did not hesitate to leave your comfortable home in Heaven and entered our world in a humble manger. You showed us God's love with your compassionate attitude and caring acts during your ministry. I am sometimes tempted by the world every day to care simply about myself and do hurtful things to people around me without any concern. I might also ignore God and the misfortunate, because I usually do not get anything concrete in return. But with your example and encouragement, I will try to be like you and follow your way of life. I will learn to love God and care about my neighbors. I will be less selfish and more generous to others without expecting anything in return. I will bring hope and joy to everyone wherever I go.

My Promise

This week I will try to be like Jesus in everything I say and do. I will not say any mean things or do any hurtful things to others for a week. I will use as many chances as possible to show Jesus to the people around me. Thank you, Jesus, My Best Friend and Savior. I love you!

FIFTH WEEK OF THE MONTH

Lord Jesus,
I Want to See...

Topic of the Week: Chosen

"Now Israel, hear the statutes and decrees which I am teaching you to observe, that you may live, and may enter in and take possession of the land which the Lord, the God of your fathers, is giving you. In your observance of the Commandments of the Lord, Your God, which I enjoin upon you, you shall not add to what I command you nor subtract from it. You have seen with your own eyes what the Lord did at Baal-peor: The Lord, Your God, destroyed from your midst everyone that followed the Baal of Peor; but you, who clung to the Lord your God, are all alive today. Therefore, I teach you the statutes and decrees as the Lord, my God, has commanded me, that you may observe them in the land you are entering to occupy. Observe them carefully, for thus will you give evidence of your wisdom and intelligence to the nations, who will hear of all these statutes and say, 'This great nation is truly a wise and intelligent people.' For what great nation is there that has gods so close to it as the Lord, our God, is to us whenever we call upon Him? Or what great nation has statutes and decrees that are as just as this whole law which I am setting before you today? However, take care and be earnestly on your guard not to forget the things which your own eyes have seen, nor let them slip from your memory as long as you live, but teach them to your children and to your children's children..." (Deuteronomy 4)

My Talk with Jesus

The Bible passage above shares with us how God has chosen God's people from the whole world to follow God's Commandments and live a certain way of life. People might be full of sins and imperfections like the rest of the world. But, God sees great potential in them for holiness and has called them from the rest of the world to witness God's love and presence. God has always watched over them and given them special treatment throughout our human history, including blessing them with the Promised Land.

We all have certain people in our lives who we respect and consider special because of the way they influence us. These folks could be our parents, siblings, friends, teachers, coaches, clergy, and so on. We have picked such people out of the crowd around us to be special people in our lives. They certainly have helped us and influenced us in a positive way. Although we might not have done anything to be considered special in God's eyes, God has chosen us to be His people and has given us special treatment over the rest of the world. In return, God calls us to follow His Laws and witness His way of life to the world. We feel honored and special for being entrusted with such tasks.

Lord Jesus, I want to see

Jesus, My Lord and Special Friend, you chose us to be God's people before the world was created. You have done many special things for us, including offering your life on the Cross to save us. I certainly have done nothing to deserve that special treatment. If anything, I have done lots of sinful things that have hurt you and damaged my relationship with you. I am truly sorry for that and am humbled for the honor you have given me. I need to do more to show you that I am worthy of the trust and love you have for me. I must live up to your Laws and Commandments to deserve to be called among your chosen people. I should witness more of your love and mercy to the world so that people may come to you and experience your divine blessings.

My Promise

This week I will give thanks to you, Lord, in prayer for calling me to be a Christian and for all your wonderful blessings. I also need to make a pledge to follow your Commandments and do only the right things to honor you this week. Thank you, Jesus, My Lord and Special Friend. I love you!

Topic of the Week: Patience

"Put on then, as God's chosen ones, holy and beloved, heartfelt compassion, kindness, humility, gentleness, and patience, bearing with one another and forgiving one another, if one has a grievance against another; as the Lord has forgiven you, so must you also do. And over all these put on love, that is, the bond of perfection. And let the peace of Christ control your hearts, the peace into which you were also called in one body. And be thankful. Let the Word of Christ dwell in you richly, as in all wisdom you teach and admonish one another, singing psalms, hymns, and spiritual songs with gratitude in your hearts to God. And whatever you do, in word or in deed, do everything in the name of the Lord Jesus, giving thanks to God the Father through Him." (Colossians 3:12-17)

My Talk with Jesus

Patience is one the virtues that many of us find it difficult to practice well daily. All of us are impulsive, and we often want to have things our way, right away. We do not like to wait for anything too long. When we are hungry and our parents tell us to wait patiently for dinner, we become very anxious and try to find anything to snack on before the meal. Or, if our families tell us to wait patiently before we open our Christmas gifts, we might find that message difficult to obey. Yet, if we can train ourselves to be patient, this great virtue will serve us well in the long run.

Again, it is tough for us to be patient when we live in a time of lightning-fast advances in technology and demands for instant solutions. People do not like to sit around and wait for their prayers to be answered. They want their prayers to be answered now! Or, our families might have some problem with money or other things to fulfill all our needs, and they want us to wait patiently on our requests so they have time to think of solutions. But, often we get mad at them for not granting our requests immediately, and we throw a tantrum. Or, when our parents or teachers ask us to wait patiently for our turn for something, we find it extremely difficult and become restless while waiting. If we can learn to be patient, we know how to let God answer our prayers in God's own time. We try to take time to pray over an important decision or think carefully about something before we say it out loud. Also, we should think twice about how we should act to avoid hurting others. These are some of the benefits that patience could bring us.

Lord Jesus, I want to see

Jesus, Gentle and Kind Shepherd, you controlled yourself many times when religious leaders attacked you and annoyed you. You also had to repeat and reveal yourself over and over to your disciples because they did understand. Without the virtue of patience, you would be very angry at your disciples and yell at the religious leaders constantly. I can learn from you and other saints to be patient in dealing with my family and friends. I can try to be kind and forgiving to people around me instead of being upset with them when they do not do things the way I want. Being patient also means that I need to learn to listen to God and others much better. I need to take time to pray and think about everything before I say or do. If I can train myself to be more patient and help others do the same, I am sure our world will be a much more peaceful and loving place.

My Promise

This week I promise not to nag my parents or fight with my siblings and friends. Instead, I will try to act patiently and let them do things their way without getting all wound up about it. I will also learn to forgive others more, just as you have done for me. Thank you, Jesus, Gentle and Kind Shepherd. I love you!

Topic of the Week: Dreams

"Jesus said to His disciples: 'Do not let your hearts be troubled. You have faith in God; have faith also in me. In my Father's house there are many dwelling places. If there were not, would I have told you that I am going to prepare a place for you? And if I go and prepare a place for you, I will come back again and take you to myself, so that where I am you also may be. Where I am going you know the way.' Thomas said to Him, 'Master, we do not know where you are going; how can we know the way?' Jesus said to Him, 'I am the way, the truth, and the life. No one comes to the Father except through me.' ... Philip said to Him, 'Master, show us the Father, and that will be enough for us.' Jesus said to him, 'Have I been with you for so long a time and you still do not know me, Philip? Whoever has seen me has seen the Father...'" (John 14:1-14)

My Talk with Jesus

As a child, we all dream of accomplishing certain things when we grow up. Some of us want to become doctors and nurses so that we can heal and bring new life to the suffering and the sick. Others might wish to be teachers and counselors to pass on knowledge and wisdom to future generations. Some might dream of working with their hands like farming, while others dream to spend their whole life doing missionary work and helping misfortunate folks.

Dreams are goals that we want to achieve in the future. Without dreams and hopes, we may end up with a boring life and never long for something better. If we do not hope to get better grades in school, we will never be able to achieve any A in our classes. If we humans did not dream of flying high or going across the sea, we would never have an airplane or ship. If we did not wish to have a convenient lifestyle, we would never have telephones, radios, televisions, computers, and other technology. If we do not dream about something, nothing spectacular will ever happen for us.

That is why we the believers have dreamt about Heaven and hoped to see God the Father since the beginning. For we know that Heaven is the place where there will be true happiness, peace, and eternal life. The Bible passage above explains that Christian dream, as Jesus the Son of God prepared to return to Heaven and be with God the Father. His disciples were sad and troubled about His departure. But, He assured them that He was returning to Heaven to prepare a place for them and wished to see them again someday. So, we the believers must dream about Heaven and God the Father if we want that dream to come true for us some day.

Lord Jesus, I want to see

Jesus, My Hope and Strength, with your Good News and hopeful teachings, you have renewed the dream for thousands of people who have felt lost and rejected in this world. You have also encouraged people to start dreaming so that wonderful things can come true for them. I might not realize how important it is to dream more and dream often. Or, I might not understand why I should dream about Heaven and eternal life. But, with your help and encouragement, I need to start dreaming about Heaven, eternal life, and other wonderful spiritual things. That way, you may have those dreams come true for me on the Last Day.

My Promise

This week I will spend some time imagining what my life in Heaven might be like and all the people that I want to meet in Heaven. I hope a couple of these people will be God the Father and Jesus, God the Son. Thank you, Jesus, My Hope and Strength. I love you!

Topic of the Week: Come True

"... When the seven years of abundance enjoyed by the land of Egypt came to an end, the seven years of famine set in, just as Joseph had predicted. Although there was famine in all the other countries, food was available throughout the land of Egypt. When hunger came to be felt throughout the land of Egypt and the people cried to Pharaoh for bread, Pharaoh directed all the Egyptians to go to Joseph and do whatever he told them. When the famine had spread throughout the land, Joseph opened all the cities that had grain and rationed it to the Egyptians since the famine had gripped the land of Egypt. In fact, the whole world came to Joseph to obtain rations of grain, for famine had gripped the whole world." (Genesis 41)

My Talk with Jesus

We all have dreams, and we look forward to seeing them come true for us. We believe in certain predictions, and we pray for them to become a reality for us. It is like we are hoping to get certain gifts for our birthdays or Christmas, and we cannot wait to open them. Or, we are dreaming of being part of some group of kids, and we look forward to seeing them welcome us into their circle. The point is that it is one thing for us to dream and believe in something. It is another thing for us to see that dream or hope to come true.

The Bible passage above reminds us of the predictions that Joseph made for Egypt and its neighboring countries. Apparently, the Lord gave Joseph an ability to see what was going to happen in the near future and interpret dreams. Particularly, he saw the upcoming famine for Egypt and the region around it due to drought and other natural phenomenon. So, he predicted that there would be a severe famine and warned the whole region about it. Thankfully, the king and leaders of Egypt listened to Joseph's prediction and warning. They began to stock up grain and other necessities to prepare for the difficult days ahead. While waiting for those days, the leaders of Egypt and Joseph must have wondered if those predictions would ever come true. This was a tense and anguished time. Thankfully, his predictions came true, and Egypt was ready to deal with it.

We Christians have an important dream and cannot wait for it to come true—we want to see God face-to-face and enjoy eternal life in the Kingdom of Heaven. While waiting for that dream to come true, we can be full of worries and anxieties. We wonder when that dream will become a reality. During this waiting time, some Christians begin to lose faith in the Christian dream and slowly abandon it. We Christians must have faith in Jesus and that dream.

Lord Jesus, I want to see

Jesus, My Dream and Best Friend, you made the dream of the Messiah and salvation for God's people come true when you entered our world. Everything that God's people and the prophets had hoped for came true with you. I might have some doubt about Heaven, eternal life, and my soul due to the bad influences of the world. But with your love and support, I will slowly erase those doubts and commit myself totally to believe in the Christian dream. I will look forward to the day when it will fully be revealed and come true. I will jump for joy and have the biggest smile when that happens.

My Promise

This week I will look back on some of my dreams or hopes and determine if I can make one of them come true. Perhaps I can work hard to get all A's on my next report card and make my dream of being on the Principal's List come true. Thank you, Jesus, My Dream and Best Friend. I love you!

MONTHLY INDEX OF TOPICS

January:	February:	March:	April:
1. Children	1. Evil	1. Betrayal	1. Hope
2. Healing	2. Forgiveness	2. Denial	2. Mercy
3. Prayer	3. Temptation	3. The Cross	3. Love
4. Sharing	4. Sorrow	4. Service	4. Hate

May:	June:	July:	August:
1. Counsel	1. Disobedience	1. Bravery	1. Daring
2. Creation	2. Fighting	2. Trials	2. Jealousy
3. Anger	3. Calmness	3. Lost	3. Faith
4. Generosity	4. Goodness	4. Hospitality	4. Holiness

September:	October:	November:	December:
1. Friendship	1. Cheating	1. Promise	1. Angel
2. Hardships	2. Failure	2. Care	2. Darkness
3. Teaching	3. Listening	3. Thankfulness	3. Light
4. Wisdom	4. Help	4. Home	4. Jesus

Fifth Week:
1. Chosen
2. Patience
3. Dreams
4. Come true

CPSIA information can be obtained
at www.ICGtesting.com
Printed in the USA
FFOW02n2339290817
39386FF